PRACTICE MAKES PERFECT®

Spanish Pronouns and Prepositions

PREMIUM FOURTH EDITION

Dorothy Richmond

McGraw Hill

New York   Chicago   San Francisco   Athens   London   Madrid   Mexico City
Milan   New Delhi   Singapore   Sydney   Toronto

3 4 5 6 7 8 9 10 LON 26 25 24

ISBN   978-1-260-46754-3
MHID   1-260-46754-6

e-ISBN   978-1-260-46755-0
e-MHID   1-260-46755-4

Interior design by Village Bookworks, Inc.

McGraw Hill products are available at special quantity discounts to use as premiums and sales promotions or for use in corporate training programs. To contact a representative, please visit the Contact Us pages at www.mhprofessional.com.

McGraw Hill Language Lab App
Audio recordings and flashcards are available to support your study of this book. Go to mhlanguagelab.com to access the online version of this application, or to locate links to the mobile app for iOS and Android devices. More details about the features of the app are available on the inside front and back covers.

Other titles by Dorothy Richmond:
Practice Makes Perfect: Basic Spanish
Practice Makes Perfect: Spanish Verb Tenses
Practice Makes Perfect: Spanish Vocabulary
Practice Makes Perfect: Spanish Vocabulary Building with Suffixes

To Daisy Richmond and Lily Richmond, the greatest loves of my life

Contents

Preface

Pronouns and prepositions are two aspects of language study that often fall through the cracks. It is not unusual to encounter individuals who have studied Spanish for years and whose vocabulary and ability to conjugate verbs are impressive, yet who trip over pronouns, unable to distinguish between direct and indirect object pronouns, and who don't really "get" **para** and **por**.

To say that Spanish pronouns and prepositions are undertaught and underlearned is an understatement. Mastery of them is essential for all students who desire to communicate with native speakers of Spanish or who simply wish to absorb the wealth of literature—from the classics to the latest fan magazines—in Spanish. Though vastly different on the surface, mastery of both requires meticulous attention to detail, careful study of both vocabulary and theory, and almost endless repetitive practice and use, until that magic moment when one simply uses pronouns and prepositions without thought, without effort, without regret for the time and energy spent learning them.

Current books on the market invariably fall short of providing sufficient discussion, examples, and exercises that allow the student to properly learn how to work with Spanish pronouns and prepositions. *Practice Makes Perfect: Spanish Pronouns and Prepositions* meets the need for explaining and practicing these two vital parts of speech.

The challenge of this text, for both the author and the student, is to take on these two very important, yet often ignored, aspects of the Spanish language. For every student who takes this challenge, I offer you congratulations and wish you great academic fortune.

Acknowledgments

It is a great honor to have a textbook go into subsequent editions because it means that the book has done its intended job well. Thus, my first thanks go to the many students who made such extensive and productive use of the previous editions of *Pronouns and Prepositions* that another edition was warranted.

As ever, I am happy to be working with Christopher Brown, my longtime editor, publisher, and friend at McGraw-Hill who oversaw the production of this book and with whom I've worked on several titles. I am ever grateful for Christopher's intelligence, attention to detail, and kindness.

My daughters, Daisy and Lily Richmond, continue to inspire and challenge me in all ways significant.

Introduction

In order to work with any system—a software program, a car, an organization, or a language—one must know its constituent parts, how to use them, and what each part means and contributes to the whole. This book deals primarily with Spanish pronouns and prepositions, which are crucial to the Spanish language system.

What is a pronoun?

A pronoun replaces an understood noun. Therefore, in order to use a pronoun, the speaker/writer and listener/reader must already be in agreement on what or whom the noun refers to. If you breeze into a room and announce, "I saw him last night," you will be greeted by blank stares and the question "Whom did you see?" On the other hand, if you made this same announcement after you and your friends had been talking about the ghost of Elvis, you still might get some stares, but everyone would understand whom you meant. And being understood—putting what is going on in your mind into someone else's mind—is the essence and aim of all communication.

Pronouns allow us to streamline our conversations: they make our conversations less wordy, but more interesting. As you begin to work with Spanish pronouns, you may at times find them frustrating, even overwhelming. Keep going. They take time to learn, and other books currently on the market do not give them enough attention, nor do these texts offer students sufficient explanations, examples, and exercises.

Part I of *Practice Makes Perfect: Spanish Pronouns and Prepositions* offers you 14 chapters about pronouns in Spanish, from the everyday subject pronoun to the specialized reciprocal pronoun. Each chapter contains an abundance of explanations, examples, and exercises. (You'll find answers to all the exercises at the back of the book.)

What is a preposition?

A preposition reveals a relationship, typically between two nouns or pronouns. This relationship may be one of place, time, direction, manner, or connection.

It is difficult to say or write much of importance or clarity without using prepositions. It is even harder to "fake it" when you don't know the correct preposition to use. Nouns and verbs often have synonyms, or you can describe them in other terms or even just point to or demonstrate "à la charades." Prepositions, however, usually have no substitutes, and it is crucial to know prepositions in order to get your point across.

Imagine trying to say "Jake lives with Matthew" in Spanish if you don't know the word for "with." Or "I have gifts for Daisy and Lily" if you don't know how to say "for." "To the right of," "to the left of," "in front of," and so on—all these prepositions need to be learned and mastered in order to be a confident, comfortable speaker of Spanish.

Prepositions are brought out in all their glory and forms in the three chapters of Part II of *Practice Makes Perfect: Spanish Pronouns and Prepositions*. In the first chapter, you are presented with the basic vocabulary and multiple uses of prepositions, as well as the sometimes subtle differences among certain prepositions that may appear to be interchangeable at first. The second chapter is devoted to **para** and **por**, two prepositions with frequently similar meanings, but distinct uses. In the third chapter, you will learn about the special relationship that many prepositions have with verbs.

Each chapter in Part II contains detailed explanations of the material, followed by examples and exercises. (Answers to these exercises, too, can be found at the end of the text.)

The appendices contain concise explanations and summaries, along with valuable charts, that provide the basis for your study of Spanish pronouns and prepositions. For example, Appendix A, "The Eight Parts of Speech," arms you with the grammatical terms you need and gives you the ability to identify all eight parts of speech when working with the language. Appendixes B and C provide comprehensive summaries that can serve as reference tools.

I sincerely hope that this text will help those who study Spanish, at any level, to achieve (and maybe surpass?) their goals of speaking, writing, and reading this incredibly rich language with greater competence and confidence. Enjoy the language. Play with it. Work with it. Make it a part of you. *¡Buena suerte!*

PRONOUNS

Subject Pronouns

FUNCTION	To replace a noun that names the subject (the actor) in a clause or sentence
SPANISH PLACEMENT	At the beginning of a clause or sentence; before the verb
ENGLISH EQUIVALENTS	"I," "you," "he," "she," "it," "we," "they"

Pronouns replace nouns that are understood either because of previous use or from context. In English, there are seven subject pronouns (also called personal pronouns): "I," "you," "he," "she," "it," "we," and "they." In Spanish, there are twelve. The difference is due to two pronouns that take gender (**nosotros** and **vosotros**) and four pronouns in Spanish for the single English pronoun "you."

SINGULAR		PLURAL	
yo	*I*	nosotros	*we* (masc., masc. & fem.)
		nosotras	*we* (fem.)
tú	*you* (informal)	vosotros	*you* (informal, masc., masc. & fem.)
		vosotras	*you* (informal, fem.)
él	*he*	ellos	*they* (masc., masc. & fem.)
ella	*she*	ellas	*they* (fem.)
usted	*you* (formal)	ustedes	*you* (formal)

Note that the pronouns for Spanish "you" differ from those for English "you" in some significant ways:

1. The pronouns **usted** and **ustedes** are often abbreviated in text. **Ud.** or **Vd.** is used for **usted**; **Uds.** or **Vds.** is used for **ustedes**.

2. The informal plural **vosotros** form is used primarily in Peninsular Spanish (Spain), while throughout Latin America, **ustedes** is used in both formal and informal situations.

The subject pronoun replaces the noun that names the subject (the actor) in a sentence, and the conjugated verb must agree in number with that subject. The Spanish regular verb endings are given below. Use this chart of verb endings together with the preceding chart of subject pronouns to help you do the first exercise.

-ar		**-er**		**-ir**	
-o	-amos	-o	-emos	-o	-imos
-as	-áis	-es	-éis	-es	-ís
-a	-an	-e	-en	-e	-en

Complete each of the following clauses with the correct subject pronoun. All of the verbs used below are regular -**ar**, -**er**, or -**ir** verbs.

1. _____ hablo

2. _____ comemos

3. _____ viven

4. _____ canta

5. _____ abrís

6. _____ vendemos

7. _____ escribe

8. _____ describen

9. _____ practicáis

10. _____ estudias

11. _____ ama

12. _____ sufro

13. _____ bebes

14. _____ tomáis

15. _____ lee

16. _____ creo

17. _____ llegas

18. _____ comprendemos

19. _____ trabajan

20. _____ miras

The use of subject pronouns in Spanish—when and how they are used—differs from English usage, even when the referent is clearly the same.

1. It is often not necessary to state or write the subject pronoun in Spanish, because the conjugated form of the verb indicates the subject (for example, the verb ending -**o** signifies the subject pronoun **yo**). In English, however, we must include the subject pronoun with the verb. In Spanish, it is only necessary to include the subject pronoun for one of the following reasons.

   a. *Clarity.* Including the subject pronoun in the third person allows you to differentiate between **él** and **ella** or **ellos/ellas** and **ustedes**.

Él es portugués y **ella** es mexicana.	*He is Portuguese and she is Mexican.*
Ellos viven en un apartamento, **ellas** viven en una casa y **ustedes** viven en un condominio.	*They* [m./m. & f.] *live in an apartment, they* [f.] *live in a house, and all of you live in a condo.*

   However, once the third-person subject has been established, there is no need to use additional subject pronouns (though it is not incorrect to use them).

Ted Kaczynski, el "Unabomber," es un sociópata y **está** en prisión condendado a cadena perpetua.	*Ted Kaczynski, the "Unabomber," is a sociopath and he is in prison for life.*
Lilia es inteligente y **trabaja** para el Departamento de Estado.	*Lily is intelligent and she works for the State Department.*

   b. *Emphasis.* To emphasize the difference between two subjects, even though they are both understood, include the subject pronoun.

¡**Yo** vivo en una casa, pero **tú** vives en un palacio!	*I live in a house, but you live in a palace!*

2. There is no Spanish word for the subject pronoun "it." When "it" (or its plural "they") is the subject of a sentence or phrase, "it" (or "they") is understood.

¿De qué color es tu casa?   What color is your house?
Es blanca.   *It is* white.

¿Dónde están los coches?   Where are the cars?
Están en el garaje.   *They are* in the garage.

EJERCICIO

1·2

Complete each phrase with either the correct subject pronoun or the correct verb ending, according to the information given. Each of the verbs below is a frequently used irregular verb.

1. _____ tengo

2. _____ tienes

3. él quier_____

4. nosotros est_____

5. vosotros sal_____

6. _____ quieren

7. yo pued_____

8. ella vien_____

9. _____ somos

10. tú sal_____

11. usted jueg_____

12. _____ pongo

13. ustedes pon_____

14. ellos dic_____

15. _____ estáis

16. _____ oyes

17. ellas pued_____

18. nosotros ve_____

19. _____ oímos

20. _____ veis

EJERCICIO

1·3

Complete each sentence with the appropriate subject pronoun, as indicated by the sentence's context or verb form.

1. Mi nombre es Miguel. _____ vivo en Minneapolis.

2. Carmen es médica y _____ trabaja en una clínica en el centro de la ciudad.

3. _____ tocamos el piano.

4. Luisa y Carlota son autores. _____ escriben libros sobre la historia de la Segunda Guerra Mundial.

5. Eres muy interesante. ¿Dónde trabajas _____?

6. Tú y tu hermanito son preciosos. ¿Dónde asistís _____ a la escuela?

7. Hola, Señor Presidente. ¿Cómo está _____?

8. LaBron James y Steph Curry son atletas famosos. _____ juegan al baloncesto.

Interrogative Pronouns

FUNCTION   To introduce a question for which the desired answer is a noun or pronoun that names a person or thing

SPANISH PLACEMENT   At the beginning of a question

ENGLISH EQUIVALENTS   "Who?" "(To) Whom?" "Whose?" "What?" "Which?"

The interrogative pronoun is used to ask a specific type of question. The answer sought is a noun or pronoun (naming either a person or a thing): "*Who* is in the soundproof booth?" "*To whom* did you send the poison pen letter?" "*Whose* dog did this?" "*What* is this?" "*Which* do you prefer?"

¿Quién? ¿Quiénes?	*Who?*
¿A quién? ¿A quiénes?	*(To) Whom?*
¿De quién? ¿De quiénes?	*Whose?*
¿Qué?	*What? Which?*
¿Cuál? ¿Cuáles?	*Which? What?*

In Spanish, **¿Qué?** often precedes a noun, and **¿Cuál?** often precedes a verb or a prepositional phrase. Note that all Spanish interrogative pronouns, with the exception of **¿Qué?**, have both a singular and a plural form. The verb must agree in number with this form.

Who? ¿Quién? ¿Quiénes?

When your question is about people, and the answer you seek involves a name or names, you ask "Who?", as in "*Who* has the cat? *John* has the cat." ("John" is the subject of the answer.) In these cases, in Spanish, use **¿Quién?** (or **¿Quiénes?** when you are seeking the names of two or more people).

Singular subject

> ¿**Quién** vive aquí?   ***Who*** *lives here?*
> Pedro Morales vive aquí.   *Pedro Morales lives here.*

Plural subject

> ¿**Quiénes** trabajan aquí?   ***Who*** *all works here?*
> Pedro y Felipe trabajan aquí. *Pedro and Felipe work here.*

With ser [sing.]

¿**Quién** es él?
Él es Pedro Morales.

Who is he?
He is Pedro Morales.

With ser [pl.]

¿**Quiénes** son ellos?
Ellos son los carpinteros.

Who are they?
They are the carpenters.

EJERCICIO
2·1

Traducción *Translate the following questions into Spanish.*

1. *Who is she?* _____

2. *Who are they [m.]?* _____

3. *Who are you [sing.]?* _____

4. *Who am I?* _____

5. *Who works here?* _____

6. *Who watches television?* _____

7. *Who speaks Spanish here?* _____

8. *Who doesn't live here?* _____

9. *Who writes the book?* _____

10. *Who is your friend?* _____

Whom? ¿A quién? ¿A quiénes?

To ask the name of a person who is the recipient of an action (as the direct object of the verb), use "Whom?", as in the sentence "*Whom do you love?*" The personal **a** must be included before the interrogative pronoun ¿**quién?** (or ¿**quiénes?** if you suspect that the answer involves more than one name).

¿**A quién** ves?
Veo a Pedro Morales.

Whom do you see?
I see Pedro Morales.

Note that the structure for use of the interrogative pronoun is parallel to that of the answer, where the **a** in the sentence **Veo a Pedro Morales** is the personal **a**.

To ask the name of a person who is the indirect recipient of an action (expressed as the object of a preposition), use the preposition **a** ("to"), as in the sentence "*To whom are you writing?*" The preposition **a** ("to") must be included before the interrogative pronoun ¿**quién?** (or ¿**quiénes?**).

¿**A quiénes** escribes?
Escribo a Pedro y a Manolo.

To whom are you writing?
I'm writing to Pedro and Manolo.

The structure for use of the interrogative pronoun is parallel to that of the answer here as well, because the **a** in the sentence **Escribo a Pedro y a Manolo** represents the English preposition "to."

NOTE The personal **a** is not used with the verbs **ser**, **estar**, and **tener**.

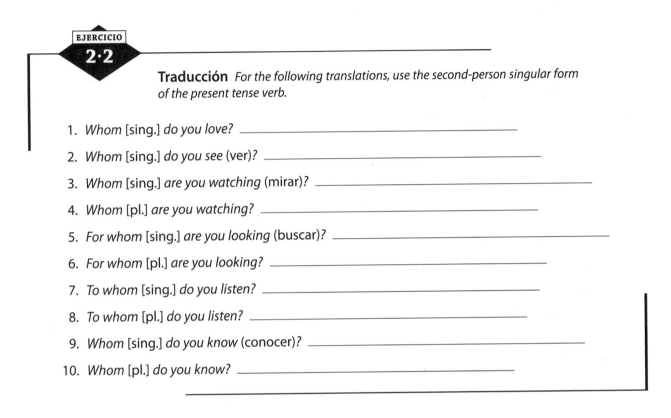

EJERCICIO
2·2

Traducción *For the following translations, use the second-person singular form of the present tense verb.*

1. *Whom* [sing.] *do you love?* _____

2. *Whom* [sing.] *do you see (ver)?* _____

3. *Whom* [sing.] *are you watching (mirar)?* _____

4. *Whom* [pl.] *are you watching?* _____

5. *For whom* [sing.] *are you looking (buscar)?* _____

6. *For whom* [pl.] *are you looking?* _____

7. *To whom* [sing.] *do you listen?* _____

8. *To whom* [pl.] *do you listen?* _____

9. *Whom* [sing.] *do you know (conocer)?* _____

10. *Whom* [pl.] *do you know?* _____

Whose? ¿De quién? ¿De quiénes?

In English, to identify the owner of something, you ask "Whose?" In Spanish, use the phrase **¿De quién?** (or **¿De quiénes?** if you think that the answer involves more than one name). In simple questions, the phrase—usually followed by a form of **ser**—is uncomplicated.

¿De quién es este libro?	***Whose*** *book is this?*
¿De quiénes son esos boletos?	***Whose*** *tickets are those?*

However, the use of the phrase does not translate directly in more complicated questions, and it is necessary to rephrase the question. For example, "Whose grandmother lives here?" becomes **¿De quién es la abuela que vive aquí?** (literally, "Of whom is the grandmother that lives here?").

¿De quién son los vecinos que no hablan inglés?	***Whose*** *neighbors don't speak English?* (lit., ***Of whom*** *are the neighbors that don't speak English?*)
¿De quién era el lápiz que pediste prestado?	***Whose*** *pencil did you borrow?* (lit., ***Of whom*** *was the pencil that you borrowed?*)
¿De quiénes son los sombreros que están en la mesa?	***Whose*** *hats are on the table?* (lit., ***Of whom*** *are the hats that are on the table?*)
¿De quiénes son los videos más populares ahora?	***Whose*** *videos are the most popular now?* (lit., ***Of whom*** *are the most popular videos now?*)

Traducción *Translate each of the following questions from English to Spanish, using singular interrogative pronouns unless otherwise indicated. The Spanish syntax is given in parentheses after the question.*

1. *Whose car is this? (Of whom is this car?)*

   _____

2. *Whose keys (la llave) are on the table? (Of whom are the keys that are on the table?)*

   _____

3. *Whose [pl.] cars are dirty? (Of whom are the cars that are dirty?)*

   _____

4. *Whose [pl.] children [f.] are reading these books? (Of whom are the children that are reading these books?)*

   _____

5. *Whose cat is drinking (beber) the milk? (Of whom is the cat that is drinking the milk?)*

   _____

6. *Whose neighbors (el vecino) live in the blue house? (Of whom are the neighbors that live in the blue house?)*

   _____

7. *Whose [pl.] students are the most intelligent? (Of whom are the most intelligent students?)*

   _____

8. *Whose car doesn't run (funcionar)? (Of whom is the car that doesn't run?)*

   _____

9. *Whose coat is this? (Of whom is this coat?)*

   _____

10. *Whose parrot (el loro) speaks Italian? (Of whom is the parrot that speaks Italian?)*

    _____

11. *Whose [pl.] CDs (el disco compacto) are these? (Of whom are these CDs?)*

    _____

12. *Whose backpack (la mochila) is that? (Of whom is that backpack?)*

    _____

For discussion of another use of "whose," see Chapter 8.

Which? ¿Qué? ¿Cuál? ¿Cuáles?

To limit a group of items or to ask someone to choose from among a number of items, you use "Which?" or "What?" in your question. In English, "Which?" generally precedes a noun ("*Which* cookbook do you want?"), while the limiting "What?" usually precedes a verb ("*What* is the best cookbook for breads?").

In Spanish, the opposite is often true. If the interrogative pronoun is followed by a noun, use **¿Qué?** If the interrogative pronoun is followed by a verb or a prepositional phrase, use **¿Cuál?** or **¿Cuáles?** In the context of **¿Cuál?** + VERB, **¿Cuál?** usually means "Which one?"

¿Qué vestido prefieres?	**Which dress** *do you prefer?*
Prefiero el vestido largo.	*I prefer the long dress.*
¿Cuál prefieres?	**Which (one)** *do you prefer?*
Prefiero el vestido largo.	*I prefer the long dress.*
¿Cuál de los vestidos prefieres?	**Which of the dresses** *do you prefer?*
Prefiero el vestido rojo.	*I prefer the red dress.*
¿Cuáles prefieres?	**Which ones** *do you prefer?*
Prefiero los zapatos negros.	*I prefer the black shoes.*
¿Cuál de las pinturas es de Miró?	**Which (one) of the paintings** *is by Miró?*
¿Qué pintura es de Miró?	**Which painting** *is by Miró?*
¿Qué número de teléfono es correcto?	**Which telephone number** *is correct?*

EJERCICIO

2·4

Traducción *Translate the following questions. Use the second-person singular Spanish form for English* you.

1. *Which book is more* (más) *interesting?* _____

2. *Which actor is more popular?* _____

3. *Which girl* (la chica) *is your cousin?* _____

4. *Which food has more fat* (la grasa)? _____

5. *Which store sells more clothing?* _____

6. *Which do you eat more, chicken* (el pollo) *or fish* (el pescado)?

   _____

7. *Which is more popular?* _____

8. *Which ones do you wear more?* _____

9. *Which shoes do you wear more?* _____

10. *Which hat is more comfortable* (cómodo)? _____

11. *Which of the hats is more comfortable?*

    _____

12. *Which program* (el programa) *do you watch?*

    _____

13. *Which [pl.] of the new programs do you watch?*

_____

14. *Which ones do you watch?* _____

¿Qué? vs. ¿Cuál?

Whether to use **¿Qué?** or **¿Cuál?** in Spanish questions confounds many speakers of English. In a nutshell, questions beginning with **¿Qué?** ask for a definition, whereas questions that begin with **¿Cuál?** ask the respondent to limit his or her answer to one of many possibilities. Consider the following questions and their literal implications as displayed in the answers:

¿Qué es tu nombre?	***What is your name?***
Mi nombre es la palabra que la gente usa cuando me llama.	*My name is the word that people use when they call to me.*
¿Cuál es tu nombre?	***What is your name?*** *(Which one of all the names that exist is yours?)*
Mi nombre es Penélope.	*My name is Penelope.*
¿Cuál es tu número de teléfono?	***What is your telephone number?*** *(Which one of the billions of telephone numbers out there is yours?)*
Mi número es (811) 555-1212.	*My number is (811) 555-1212.*

As you can see, **¿Qué?** requests a literal answer, and **¿Cuál?** asks for a selection from a large pool of possible answers.

To determine whether to use **¿Qué?** or **¿Cuál?**, consider the following:

- Generally speaking, **¿Qué?** precedes a noun and **¿Cuál?** precedes a verb.
- If you want a definition, use **¿Qué?**
- If there are many possible answers and you want to know the correct answer in a particular situation—that is, the limited answer—use **¿Cuál?**

EJERCICIO
2·5

*Mark whether you would use **¿Qué?** or **¿Cuál?** in the following questions. Then translate the questions. Use the second-person singular Spanish form for English you.*

	¿Qué?	¿Cuál?
1. *What day is today?*	☐	☐
2. *What is the date* (la fecha) *today?*	☐	☐
3. *What is his name?*	☐	☐

	¿Qué?	¿Cuál?
4. *What time* (la hora) *is it?*	☐	☐
5. *What is your reason* (la razón) *for this* (esto)?	☐	☐
6. *What is that* (eso)?	☐	☐
7. *Which book do you want?*	☐	☐
8. *Which ones do you want?*	☐	☐
9. *Which woman is your friend?*	☐	☐
10. *What does this mean* (significar)?	☐	☐
11. *What is the answer* (la respuesta)?	☐	☐
12. *What do you want to know* (saber)?	☐	☐
13. *What is your name?*	☐	☐
14. *What is your address* (la dirección)?	☐	☐

Prepositional Pronouns

FUNCTION	To replace a noun that names a person or thing following a preposition, serving as the object of that preposition
SPANISH PLACEMENT	Immediately after a preposition
ENGLISH EQUIVALENTS	"me," "you," "him," "her," "it," "us," "them"

Standard prepositional pronouns

The pronouns that follow prepositions are nearly identical to the subject pronouns. The only change comes with the first- and second-person singular forms **mí** and **ti**. In this context, **mí** takes an accent over the **i** to distinguish it from **mi**, the possessive adjective, which means "my."

SINGULAR		PLURAL	
mí	*me*	nosotros	*us* (masc., masc. & fem.)
		nosotras	*us* (fem.)
ti	*you* (informal)	vosotros	*you* (informal, masc., masc. & fem.)
		vosotras	*you* (informal, fem.)
él	*him*	ellos	*them, it* (masc.)
ella	*her, it* (fem.)	ellas	*them, it* (fem.)
usted	*you* (formal)	ustedes	*you* (formal)
ello	*it* (masc., neut.)		

Note that after a preposition, the word **ello** means "it" when the referent is an object, event, or idea that is either masculine or neuter; use **ella** for a feminine referent.

El accidente sucedió hace un año.	*The accident happened a year ago.*
Él escribió un cuento acerca de **ello**.	*He wrote a story about **it**.*
Compramos una cama nueva y tenemos las almohadas perfectas para **ella**.	*We're buying a new bed, and we have the perfect pillows for **it**.*

The following exercise includes several frequently used prepositions. For fuller discussion and a more complete vocabulary listing of prepositions, consult Part II, Prepositions.

Use these prepositions in translating the following sentences. Unless otherwise indicated, use the second-person singular Spanish form for English you.

VOCABULARIO

a la derecha de	to the right of
a la izquierda de	to the left of
acerca de	about
cerca de	near
de	from, of
debajo de	underneath
delante de	in front of; ahead of
detrás de	behind
encima de	on top of
para	for

1. He has a book for me. _____

2. I have a gift for you. _____

3. What do you have for me? _____

4. The table is from her. _____

5. I buy my books from them. _____

6. She runs ahead of us. _____

7. You are behind him. _____

8. He lives near me. _____

9. The carpet (la alfombra) is underneath us [f.].

_____

10. He lives near you [pl.]. _____

11. He writes a book about her. _____

12. We walk behind them. _____

13. She dances to the right of me. _____

14. They work to the left of you. _____

15. The food is in front of us. _____

Pronouns with con

Certain pronouns undergo some changes when they follow the preposition **con** ("with"). Those changes are as follows:

SINGULAR		PLURAL	
conmigo	*with me*	con nosotros, con nosotras	*with us*
contigo	*with you*	con vosotros, con nosotras	*with you*
consigo	*with him, with her, with you*	**consigo**	*with them, with you*

In situations where clarification is needed in the third person, the standard prepositional pronouns are used with **con** ("with"), as shown here:

con él	*with him*	con ellos	*with them*
con ella	*with her, with it*	con ellas	*with them*
con usted	*with you*	con ustedes	*with you*
con ello	*with it*		

In the first- and second-person singular, **mí** and **ti** become **conmigo** and **contigo**.

¿Por qué no vienes **conmigo** al concierto?	*Why don't you come **with me** to the concert?*
Está bien. Iré **contigo**.	*Okay. I'll go **with you**.*

In the third person (both singular and plural), **consigo** is typically used when the object of the preposition refers to the subject.

Él llevó los libros **consigo**.	*He took the books **with him**.*
Ellos llevaron los libros **consigo**.	*They took the books **with them**.*

Use **con** plus the appropriate standard prepositional pronoun when the object of the preposition refers to someone other than the subject of the sentence.

Mi hermano vive en San Diego y mi padre vive **con él**.	*My brother lives in San Diego, and my father lives **with him**.*
Mi hermano vive **con ellos**.	*My brother lives **with them**.*

In the **nosotros** and **vosotros** forms, the subject pronoun and the prepositional pronoun are identical.

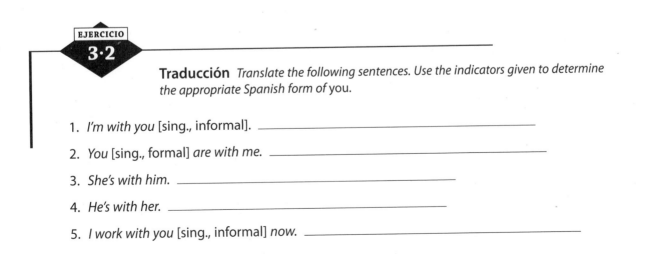

EJERCICIO
3·2

Traducción *Translate the following sentences. Use the indicators given to determine the appropriate Spanish form of* you.

1. *I'm with you* [sing., informal]. _____

2. *You* [sing., formal] *are with me.* _____

3. *She's with him.* _____

4. *He's with her.* _____

5. *I work with you* [sing., informal] *now.* _____

6. *They live with me.* _____

7. *Does she study with you* [sing., informal]? _____

8. *Who lives with you* [pl., formal]? _____

9. *Why don't you* [sing., informal) *want to work with him?*

   _____

10. *I want to speak with you* [sing., formal]. _____

11. *He lives with us.* _____

12. *She always takes the keys* (la llave) *with her.*

    _____

13. *They* [m.] *never take the keys with them.*

    _____

14. *The force* (la fuerza) *is with you.* _____

15. *Why don't you* [sing., formal] *take the umbrella* (el paraguas) *with you?*

    _____

16. *Why don't they* [f.] *take the umbrella with them?*

    _____

Subject pronouns with prepositions

There are six prepositions that take a subject pronoun—even in the first- and second-person singular—instead of the standard prepositional pronouns.

entre	*between*	menos	*except*
excepto	*except*	salvo	*except*
incluso	*including*	según	*according to*

The prepositions **excepto**, **menos**, and **salvo**, all of which mean "except," can, for the most part, be used interchangeably.

Juan está **entre tú y yo**.	Juan is **between you and me**.
Todos bailan **excepto él**.	
Todos bailan **menos él**.	*Everyone dances, **except him**.*
Todos bailan **salvo él**.	
Según él, debemos llegar pronto.	***According to him**, we should be there soon.*
Todos vamos a la fiesta, **incluso tú**.	*We're all going to the party, **including you**.*

Traducción *Translate the following sentences into Spanish. Unless otherwise indicated, use the second-person singular Spanish form for English* you.

1. *There are twenty people here, including you and me.*

_____

2. *According to her, money can buy happiness* (la felicidad).

_____

3. *Between you, me, and the grand piano* (el piano de cola), *this painting is ghastly* (espantoso).

_____

4. *I think* (creer) *that everybody* (todo el mundo) *here speaks German, except me.*

_____

5. *Between us and them, we have enough* (suficiente) *money.*

_____

6. *Everyone* (todos) *here is outraged* (escandalizado), *including me.*

_____

7. *Everyone in the neighborhood* (la vecindad) *has a swimming pool* (la piscina), *except us.*

_____

8. *We are in a lot of trouble* (tener muchas dificultades), *according to me.*

_____

9. *Everybody is ready* (listo), *except you* [sing., formal].

_____

10. *According to them, it is possible to live on Mars* (Marte).

_____

Reflexive pronouns following a preposition

When you do something for yourself, it is called a reflexive action, because the action is reflected back to the performer of the action. (For a more complete discussion of reflexive pronouns, see Chapter 11, Reflexive Object Pronouns.) A reflexive action can be expressed either with a reflexive pronoun alone or with a PREPOSITION + PRONOUN. When a preposition is used—in the examples given below, we use the preposition **a** ("to")—then the pronouns that follow the preposition are as shown below:

a mí mismo	*to myself* (masc.)	**a nosotros mismos**	*to ourselves* (masc.)
a mí misma	*to myself* (fem.)	**a nosotras mismas**	*to ourselves* (fem.)
a ti mismo	*to yourself* (masc.)	**a vosotros mismos**	*to yourselves* (masc.)
a ti misma	*to yourself* (fem.)	**a vosotras mismas**	*to yourselves* (fem.)
a sí mismo	*to himself, to yourself, to itself* (masc.)	**a sí mismos**	*to themselves, to yourselves* (masc.)
a sí misma	*to herself, to yourself, to itself* (fem.)	**a sí mismas**	*to themselves, to yourselves* (fem.)

Preparo el café **para mí mismo**.	*I prepare the coffee **for myself**.*
Marta, tú piensas solamente **en ti misma**.	*Marta, you think only **about yourself**.*
Los buenos maestros enseñan **a sí mismos** también.	*Good teachers teach **themselves** too.*

EJERCICIO
3·4

Traducción *Translate the following sentences into Spanish.*

1. *I buy the car for* (para) *myself* [m.].

   _____

2. *He does everything for* (para) *himself.*

   _____

3. *They do everything by* (por) *themselves* [m.].

   _____

4. *She hurts* (perjudicar a) *herself when she tells a lie* (la mentira).

   _____

5. *You* [f. pl., informal] *only* (sólo) *hurt yourselves.*

   _____

6. *I write notes* (la nota) *to myself* [f.] *in order to* (para) *remember* (recordar) *the things that I need to do.*

   _____

7. *You should have time for* (para) *yourself* [m.] *every day.*

   _____

8. *She always buys a gift for herself on her birthday.*

   _____

9. *When I travel, I send my purchases (la compra) to myself [f.] through the mail (por correo).*

_____

10. *You [m. sing., formal] can't sell your house to yourself. It's ridiculous!*

_____

EJERCICIO
3·5

Traducción *Translate the following paragraph into Spanish.*

VOCABULARIO

acerca de	*about*
ahora	*now*
al lado de	*next door to*
el árbol	*tree*
creer	*to believe, think*
delante de	*in front of*
después	*then*
entrar en	*to enter into*
el mapache	*raccoon*
el mundo	*world*
el oso	*bear*
salir de	*to leave from*
si	*if*
tener suerte	*to be lucky*
usualmente	*usually*

Pedro is my friend. I am very happy, because he lives next door to me. A raccoon lives underneath my house. Between you [pl.] and me, I think that raccoons are interesting animals. I'm reading a book about them now. Usually the raccoon lives in a tree, but I am lucky because my house is on top of this raccoon. According to Pedro, the raccoon is part of the bear family, and he believes that if he sees the animal in front of him, it's "goodbye, world." When Pedro leaves (from) or enters (into) my house, he always looks to the left and then to the right.

_____

_____

_____

_____

_____

_____

_____

Possessive Pronouns

FUNCTION	To replace the nouns that name the owner of an object and the object itself
SPANISH PLACEMENT	Immediately after a conjugated verb (often **ser**)
ENGLISH EQUIVALENTS	"mine," "yours," "his," "hers," "its," "ours," "theirs"

Possessive pronouns are not used as frequently in Spanish as they are in English. Because these pronouns stand for the object owned as well as the owner, they agree with the object owned in number and gender.

SINGULAR		PLURAL	
mío, míos	*mine*	nuestro, nuestros	*ours*
mía, mías	*mine*	nuestra, nuestras	*ours*
tuyo, tuyos	*yours*	vuestro, vuestros	*yours*
tuya, tuyas	*yours*	vuestra, vuestras	*yours*
suyo, suyos	*his, hers, yours, its*	suyo, suyos	*theirs, yours*
suya, suyas	*his, hers, yours, its*	suya, suyas	*theirs, yours*

The possessive pronoun differs from the possessive adjective in significant ways. The adjective modifies and precedes the noun, as in the sentence **Es *mi* gato** ("It is *my* cat"), whereas the pronoun includes the significance of the noun and follows the conjugated verb, as in the sentence **Es *mío*** ("It is *mine*"). If the noun is plural, the possessive adjective is plural as well: **mi gato**, **mis gatos**; **tu televisor**, **tus televisores**. The following chart shows the possessive adjectives.

SINGULAR		PLURAL	
mi, mis	*my*	nuestro, nuestros	*our*
		nuestra, nuestras	*our*
tu, tus	*your*	vuestro, vuestros	*your*
		vuestra, vuestras	*your*
su, sus	*his, her, your, its*	su, sus	*their, your*

Possessive pronouns following **ser**

The possessive pronoun frequently appears after the third-person conjugated forms of **ser**—**es** and **son**. The possessive pronoun takes the gender of the things owned, *not* of the owner.

¿El chaleco? **Es mío.**	The vest? ***It's mine.***
¿Las herramientas? **Son suyas.**	The tools? ***They are theirs.***

Rewrite the following sentences, using the appropriate possessive pronouns in place of the expressions that have possessive adjectives. Remember that a possessive pronoun takes the gender and number of the object owned.

1. Es mi teléfono.   Es _____.

2. Es tu hamburguesa.   Es _____.

3. Es su refrigerador.   Es _____.

4. Son mis gafas.   Son _____.

5. Son sus relojes.   Son _____.

6. Es nuestra mesa.   Es _____.

7. Son tus tazas.   Son _____.

8. Son vuestros tenedores.   Son _____.

9. Son sus sillas.   Son _____.

10. Es vuestra lámpara.   Es _____.

11. Son mis sábanas (sheets).   Son _____.

12. Son tus fundas (pillowcases).   Son _____.

13. Son nuestras colchas (quilts).   Son _____.

14. Es su pintura.   Es _____.

15. Es su teléfono celular.   Es _____.

Traducción Translate the following pairs of sentences into Spanish, using possessive pronouns.

1. *The cat* [m.] *is mine. The cats* [f.] *are mine.*

_____

2. *The snake* (la culebra) *is yours. The snakes are yours.*

_____

3. *The bird* (el pájaro) *is hers. The birds are hers.*

_____

4. *The monkey* (el mono) *is his. The monkeys are his.*

_____

5. *The giraffe* (la jirafa) *is ours. The giraffes are ours.*

_____

6. *The pig* (el cerdo) *is theirs. The pigs are theirs.*

_____

7. *The spider* (la araña) *is mine. The spiders are mine.*

_____

8. *The horse* (el caballo) *is yours. The horses are yours.*

_____

9. *The butterfly* (la mariposa) *is hers. The butterflies are hers.*

_____

10. *The elephant* (el elefante) *is ours. The elephants are ours.*

_____

Possessive pronouns expressing "of mine/yours/his/hers/ours/theirs"

When the possessive pronoun follows a noun in English, the word "of" is used before the possessive pronoun ("of mine," "of yours," "of his," "of hers," "of ours," "of theirs"). In Spanish, there is no need to add **de** ("of"). Use of the possessive pronoun immediately after a noun adds emphasis to the owner of the object. (Use of the possessive adjective usually emphasizes the object owned.)

La amiga suya es bonita.	*The friend of hers is pretty.*
El coche suyo es un clásico.	*The car of his is a classic.*
Esos compañeros míos son muy listos.	*Those classmates of mine are very clever.*

EJERCICIO
4·3

Traducción *Use the second-person singular Spanish form for English* you.

1. *A friend [m.] of mine works here.* _____

2. *A friend [f.] of mine lives here.* _____

3. *Some friends [m.] of mine have a cabin* (la cabaña) *in Canada.*

_____

4. *A friend [f.] of his studies Spanish.* _____

5. *I work with a friend [f.] of yours.* _____

6. *A colleague* (el colega) *of ours speaks German* (alemán) *and Gaelic* (gaélico).

_____

7. *They don't want to speak with him, because he is an enemy* (el enemigo) *of theirs.*

_____

8. *A friend [m.] of yours is a friend of mine.*

_____

9. *Those paintings* (la pintura) *of his are fascinating* (fascinante).

_____

10. *A cousin [f.] of ours is a princess* (la princesa) *in Europe* (Europa).

_____

Possessive pronouns in statements of comparison

In Spanish, when two or more things are compared (or contrasted), the name of the first item is mentioned, and the other items are typically referred to by pronouns. This is frequently seen in cases involving possession, as in the sentence "My house is red, but *yours* (your house) is white." In these situations, you must use the appropriate definite article with the possessive pronoun.

Su casa es roja, pero **la mía** es blanca.	*His house is red, but **mine** is white.*
Mi automóvil es francés, pero **el suyo** es italiano.	*My automobile is French, but **theirs** is Italian.*
Sus marcos son de plata, pero **los míos** son de oro.	*Her frames are silver, but **mine** are gold.*
Nuestra marca es barata; **la suya** es cara.	*Our brand is cheap; **theirs** is expensive.*

EJERCICIO
4·4

Traducción *Unless otherwise indicated, use the second-person singular Spanish form for English* you.

1. *Their house is dirty* (sucio), *but ours is clean* (limpio).

_____

2. *Her books are in the kitchen, and mine are in the dining room.*

_____

3. *He keeps* (guardar) *his money in the bank, but I keep mine under the mattress* (el colchón).

_____

4. *His cousins live in Hollywood, and hers live in Seattle.*

_____

5. *Our dog is a collie* (el perro pastor), *and hers is a poodle* (el perro de lana).

_____

6. *Her jewels* (la joya) *are fake* (la imitación), *but mine are real* (auténtico).

_____

7. *They buy their food in the supermarket* (el supermercado), *but we grow* (cultivar) *ours.*

_____

8. *His attorney* (el abogado) *works for a big firm* (la firma). *Ours has an office in a basement.*

_____

9. *It's my life. It isn't yours.*

_____

10. *You* [pl., informal] *have your problems* (el problema), *and I have mine.*

_____

Possessive pronouns with regular comparisons

Regular comparisons in Spanish use **más… que** ("more . . . than"), **menos… que** ("less . . . than"), or **tan… como** ("as . . . as").

Julia es **más alta que** Diego.   *Julia is **taller than** Diego.*
Diego es **tan guapo como** Steve Buscemi.   *Diego is **as handsome as** Steve Buscemi.*

When we compare two equally named people or things that are possessed or owned, the first one is mentioned and the second one is usually replaced by a possessive pronoun and the appropriate definite article.

Mi amigo es **más alto que el tuyo**.   *My friend is **taller than yours**.*
Mi amiga es **más interesante que la vuestra**.   *My friend is **more interesting than yours**.*
Su casa es **menos elegante que la nuestra**.   *Their house is **less elegant than ours**.*
Su gato no es **tan peludo como el mío**.   *His cat isn't **as furry as mine**.*
Mi café no está **tan sabroso como el tuyo**.   *My coffee isn't **as delicious as yours**.*

EJERCICIO
4·5

Traducción

1. *Their house is bigger than mine.*

_____

2. *My house isn't as big as theirs.*

_____

3. *Her clothing is more expensive than mine.*

_____

4. *Your* [pl., informal] *jewels* (la joya) *are more elegant than ours.*

_____

5. *Her ferret* (el hurón) *isn't as friendly* (amable) *as ours.*

_____

6. *His thermos* (el termo) *isn't as full* (lleno) *as mine.*

_____

7. *María's report* (el reportaje) *is more interesting than his.*

_____

8. *Juan's laptop* (el portatíl) *is newer than yours* [sing., formal].

_____

9. *Her envelopes* (el sobre) *are prettier than mine. I'm going to buy a box* (la caja).

_____

10. *Their hammers* (el martillo) *aren't as heavy* (pesado) *as yours* [sing., informal].

_____

Possessive pronouns with irregular comparatives

There are four irregular adjectives of comparison:

mejor, mejores	*better*	mayor, mayores	*older*
peor, peores	*worse*	menor, menores	*younger*

The Spanish syntax for sentences with these irregular comparatives is identical to English syntax. Note that while these irregular comparatives do not take gender, they do agree in number with the subject of the sentence.

Mi tortuga **es mejor** que la tuya.	*My turtle **is better** than yours.*
Mis tortugas **son mejores** que las tuyas.	*My turtles **are better** than yours.*
Su oso **es peor** que el nuestro.	*His bear **is worse** than ours.*
Sus osos **son peores** que los nuestros.	*His bears **are worse** than ours.*
Su gorila **es mayor** que el tuyo.	*His gorilla **is older** than yours.*
Sus gorilas **son mayores** que los tuyos.	*His gorillas **are older** than yours.*
Tu mosca **es menor** que la mía.	*Your fly **is younger** than mine.*
Tus moscas **son menores** que las mías.	*Your flies **are younger** than mine.*

Traducción

1. *Your* [sing., informal] *car is better than mine.*

_____

2. *Their chairs are better than ours.*

_____

3. *My painting is worse than his.*

_____

4. *Elena's curtains* (las cortinas) *are worse than his.*

_____

5. *Your* [sing., formal] *friend is older than mine.*

_____

6. *My grandparents are older than yours* [sing., informal].

_____

7. *Our son is younger than yours* [pl., informal].

_____

8. *Our goldfish* (la carpa dorada) *are younger than theirs.*

_____

9. *Julia's paella is better than mine.*

_____

10. *Beethoven's music* (la música) *is better than hers.*

_____

EJERCICIO
4·7

Traducción

VOCABULARIO

el anillo	*ring*
el candelabro	*candelabra*
el cleptómano, la cleptómana	*kleptomaniac*
la cosa	*thing*
disgustado, disgustada	*upset*
Figúrate	*Go figure*
hasta	*even*
las iniciales	*initials*
la lavadora	*washer*
la ley	*law*
nada	*nothing*
la pintura	*painting*
el por ciento	*percent*
por eso	*therefore*
la posesión	*possession*
el refrigerador	*refrigerator*
el reloj de péndulo	*grandfather clock*
la secadora	*dryer*
todo	*everything*

I am very upset because Silvia has my ring. She says that it is hers, but I know that it is mine because it has my initials. Silvia is a kleptomaniac. Nothing in her house is hers. Many things are mine. For example, all the paintings are mine, the grandfather clock is mine, the candelabra in the dining room is mine, the washer and dryer are mine, even the food in the refrigerator is mine. What can I do? The famous lawyer Perry Mason (of classic television) says that possession is ninety-nine percent of the law. Therefore, everything is hers. Go figure!

Demonstrative Pronouns

FUNCTION: To replace an understood noun and point out its location relative to the speaker

SPANISH PLACEMENT: Before the verb (when used as a subject) OR immediately after the verb (when used as an object)

ENGLISH EQUIVALENTS: "this (one)," "that (one)," "these (ones)," "those (ones)"

The pronouns in the following chart may look familiar to you, because they are identical to demonstrative adjectives, except that the demonstrative pronouns take an accent mark. Think of it like this: if you drop the noun, the demonstrative adjective picks up an accent mark and becomes a demonstrative pronoun.

The exception to this rule is the neuter forms: **esto**, **eso**, and **aquello**. These forms are discussed later.

	MASCULINE	FEMININE	NEUTER
this (one)	éste	ésta	esto
these (ones)	éstos	éstas	
that (one)	ése	ésa	eso
those (ones)	ésos	ésas	
that over there	aquél	aquélla	aquello
those over there	aquéllos	aquéllas	

Demonstrative pronouns with gender

When the pronoun refers to and includes the significance of something in particular, the gender and number of that referent are reflected in the pronoun.

Este coche es mío, pero **ése** es suyo.
La mejor marca es **ésta**.
Estas ventanas están limpias, pero **ésas** todavía faltan por limpiar.
Aquellas mesas son de roble, **ésas** son de pino y **éstas** son de caoba.

*This car is mine, but **that one** is his.*
*The best brand is **this one**.*
*These windows are clean, but **those** still need to be cleaned.*
*Those tables over there are oak, **those** are pine, and **these** are mahogany.*

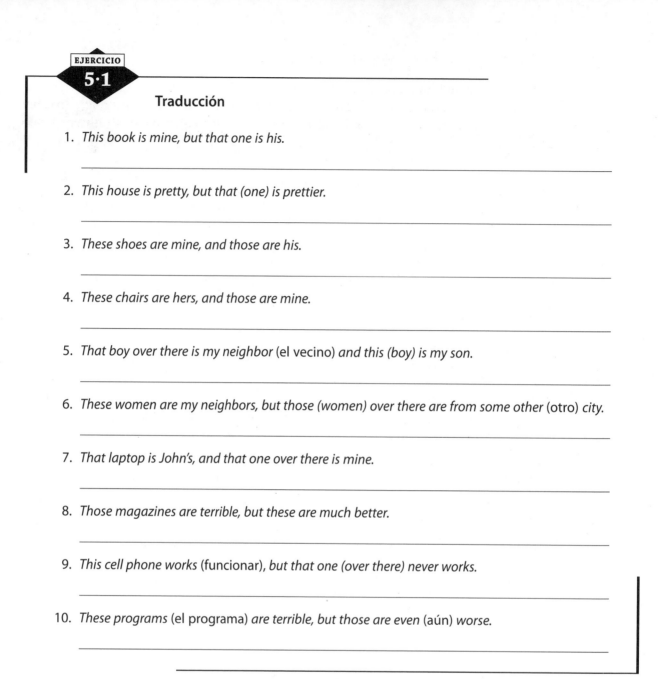

Traducción

1. *This book is mine, but that one is his.*

   _____

2. *This house is pretty, but that (one) is prettier.*

   _____

3. *These shoes are mine, and those are his.*

   _____

4. *These chairs are hers, and those are mine.*

   _____

5. *That boy over there is my neighbor* (el vecino) *and this (boy) is my son.*

   _____

6. *These women are my neighbors, but those (women) over there are from some other* (otro) *city.*

   _____

7. *That laptop is John's, and that one over there is mine.*

   _____

8. *Those magazines are terrible, but these are much better.*

   _____

9. *This cell phone works* (funcionar), *but that one (over there) never works.*

   _____

10. *These programs* (el programa) *are terrible, but those are even* (aún) *worse.*

    _____

Neuter demonstrative pronouns

In Spanish, to refer to something nonspecific ("*That's* not true!") or when you don't know or can't express the name of the referent ("What is *this*?"), use the neuter demonstrative pronoun. In other words, if there is no direct referent (so that it cannot be stated), the neuter demonstrative pronoun must be used.

The neuter demonstrative pronouns follow:

esto   *this*   eso   *that*   aquello   *that over there*

Demonstrative pronouns are generally used in exclamations, questions, and abstractions.

¡**Esto** es absurdo!	***This*** *is absurd!*
¿Qué es **eso**?	*What is **that**?*
Aquello es una monstruosidad.	***That*** *(unspecified thing far away) is a monstrosity.*
No tengo dinero, por **eso** no puedo ir.	*I don't have any money, **therefore** (lit., for that) I can't go.*

EJERCICIO

5·2

Traducción

1. *This is great!* _____

2. *What is this?* _____

3. *That is a crime* (el crimen). _____

4. *I never do that.* _____

5. *This is a sin* (el pecado). _____

6. *What is happening* (pasar) *with that (thing far away)?*

   _____

7. *That is why you* [sing., informal] *should vote.* _____

8. *This is why I shouldn't smoke.* _____

9. *Who says that?* _____

10. *Who writes this?* _____

11. *Who has that?* _____

12. *Why do they do this?* _____

Traducción

VOCABULARIO		
	a menudo	*often*
	la actitud	*attitude*
	la clase	*class*
	desgraciadamente	*unfortunately*
	espero que sí	*I hope so*
	estúpido	*stupid*
	frustrado, frustrada	*frustrated*
	la graduación	*graduation*
	el profesora, la profesora	*professor*
	quizás	*maybe*
	la tarea	*assignment*
	terminar	*to end*
	el trabajo	*job*
	la vida es lo que tú haces de ella	*life is what you make it*

"Who needs this? This is so stupid! I don't need this for my job." Some people say this when they are frustrated or when they have to take a class at (en) the university that they don't want to take. It's this class or that one. It's this professor or that one. It's these books or those. It's these assignments or those. When does this end? Does this end after graduation? Maybe. I hope so. This is not a productive attitude. Life is what you make it.

_____

_____

_____

_____

_____

_____

_____

Numbers as Pronouns

FUNCTION	To replace an understood or omitted noun, assuming the meaning of the noun itself as well as the number
SPANISH PLACEMENT	Before the verb (when used as a subject) OR after the verb (when used as an object)
ENGLISH EQUIVALENTS	Cardinal numbers: "one," "two," "three," etc.
	Ordinal numbers: "first," "second," "third," etc.

Numbers function as pronouns when they stand for a noun that is understood or has been omitted as well as the number itself. Both cardinal and ordinal numbers serve this function.

CARDINAL NUMBERS	ORDINAL NUMBERS
uno, una	primero, primera
dos	segundo, segunda
tres	tercero, tercera
cuatro	cuarto, cuarta
cinco	quinto, quinta
seis	sexto, sexta
siete	séptimo, séptima
ocho	octavo, octava
nueve	noveno, novena
diez	décimo, décima

The cardinal numbers continue into infinity. However, after **décimo** ("tenth"), the ordinal forms offer two possibilities: Continue in the pattern with ordinal numbers—**onceavo** ("eleventh"), **doceavo** ("twelfth"), **treceavo** ("thirteenth"), etc.—or, more commonly, use the cardinal number either alone or placed after the noun.

Quiero **el décimo**.	*I want **the tenth one**.*
Quiero **el doceavo**. Quiero **el doce**.	*I want **the twelfth one**.*
Vivo en **el onceavo piso**. Vivo en **el (piso) once**.	*I live on **the eleventh (floor)**.*

Cardinal numbers as pronouns

When used as pronouns, cardinal numbers include the significance of the understood noun, for example, "How many children do you have? I have *three*." In this case, "three" represents "three children." Remember that when you use the number **uno** ("one") as a pronoun, it changes to **una** when replacing a feminine noun.

¿Cuántos libros lees tú al año?　　How many books do you read each year?
　　Leo **uno**.　　　　　　　　　　I read **one**.
¿Estas galletas son para la fiesta?　These cookies are for the party?
　　Pues, sólo comí **una**.　　　　Well, I only ate **one**.

EJERCICIO
6·1

Traducción *Unless otherwise indicated, use the second-person singular Spanish form for English* you.

1. *How many cars do you have? I have one.*

2. *How many houses do you have? I have one.*

3. *How many cookies do you want? I want ten.*

4. *How many hamburgers do you [pl., formal] want? Jane wants two and I want one.*

5. *How many people are there in your family? There are three.*

6. *He has seven dogs, but I only have six.*

7. *He sees many stars* (la estrella) *in the sky* (el cielo), *but I see only one.*

8. *Maria knows* (conocer) *all these paintings* (la pintura), *but we know only one.*

9. *I have only one chair, but one is better than nothing.*

10. *How many cards* (el naipe) *do you want? I want one.*

Ordinal numbers as pronouns

When an ordinal number serves as an adjective, it precedes the noun and agrees with it in number and gender. The noun in these cases is always in its singular form: **el segundo libro**, **la segunda iglesia**.

   If the noun is omitted, the ordinal number serves instead as a pronoun. The meaning of the noun is then understood, its gender is shown by the **-o** or **-a** ending, and the article is retained: **el segundo libro** becomes **el segundo**.

Tienes el primer libro y el tercer libro, y yo tengo **el segundo**.	You have the first book and the third book, and I have **the second**.
Febrero es el segundo mes y enero es **el primero**.	February is the second month, and January is **the first**.
Ella vive en la cuarta casa y él vive en **la quinta**.	She lives in the fourth house, and he lives in **the fifth**.

Note that as adjectives, the ordinals **primero** and **tercero** drop the **-o** when preceding a masculine singular noun: **el primer libro**, **el tercer libro**. As a pronoun, the **-o** ending is retained: **el primero**, **el tercero**.

EJERCICIO

6·2

Based on the numbered order of the pictures, complete each sentence with the appropriate ordinal pronoun. The first item has been done for you.

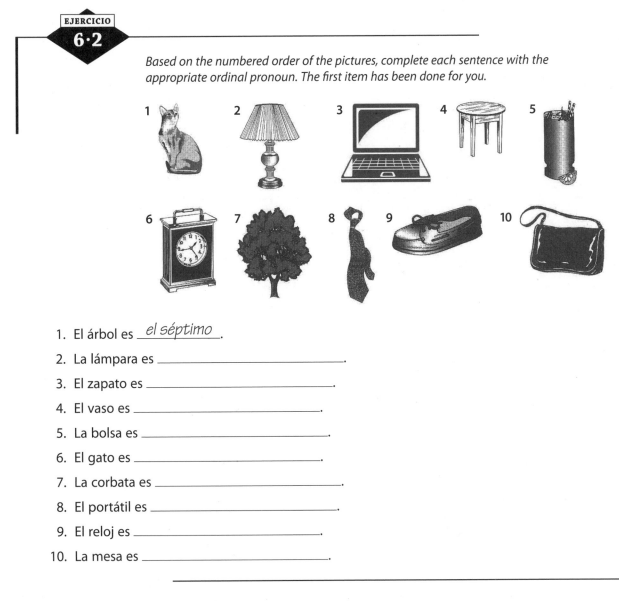

1. El árbol es _el séptimo_.

2. La lámpara es _____.

3. El zapato es _____.

4. El vaso es _____.

5. La bolsa es _____.

6. El gato es _____.

7. La corbata es _____.

8. El portátil es _____.

9. El reloj es _____.

10. La mesa es _____.

Traducción

1. *I live in the second house on the left* (a la izquierda), *and Miguel lives in the sixth.*

   _____

2. *Who lives in the eighth house? I don't know, but Marcos lives in the seventh.*

   _____

3. *My car is the third (one) on the right* (a la derecha), *and Ricardo's car is the fourth (one).*

   _____

4. *The Bible says that Adam* (Adán) *is the first person* (la persona) *and that Eve* (Eva) *is the second.*

   _____

5. *The first movie* (la película) *usually is better than* (mejor que) *the second.*

   _____

6. *The actor's third movie is better than the fourth.*

   _____

7. *His fifth book is more interesting than the sixth.*

   _____

8. *In Spain, the first day of the week is Monday, and the seventh is Sunday.*

   _____

9. *The eighth month is August, the ninth is September, and the tenth is October.*

   _____

10. *The first puzzle* (el rompecabezas) *is harder* (más difícil) *than the second.*

    _____

11. *Today is the first (day) of autumn.*

    _____

12. *The first time* (la vez) *is always better than the second, the third, and so on* (y así sucesivamente).

    _____

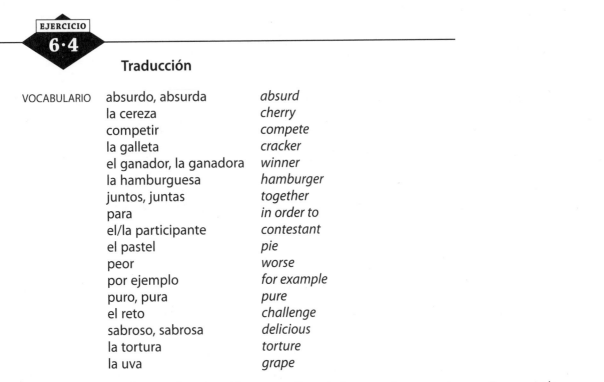

Traducción

VOCABULARIO

absurdo, absurda	*absurd*
la cereza	*cherry*
competir	*compete*
la galleta	*cracker*
el ganador, la ganadora	*winner*
la hamburguesa	*hamburger*
juntos, juntas	*together*
para	*in order to*
el/la participante	*contestant*
el pastel	*pie*
peor	*worse*
por ejemplo	*for example*
puro, pura	*pure*
el reto	*challenge*
sabroso, sabrosa	*delicious*
la tortura	*torture*
la uva	*grape*

When we eat together, my friend and I compete (in order) to see who can eat more. For example, when we eat crackers, if I eat one, he eats two. Then I eat three, and he eats four. The first contestant with an empty plate is the winner. This is easy with crackers or grapes or cherries. But it is very difficult with hamburgers. The first is delicious. The second, too. The third is not bad. The fourth is a challenge. The fifth is absurd—also the sixth, the seventh, and the eighth. The ninth is pure torture. And the tenth is impossible. It's worse with pies!

Adjective Pronouns

FUNCTION	To assume the meaning of an understood, irrelevant, or omitted noun
SPANISH PLACEMENT	Before the verb (when used as a subject) OR after the verb (when used as an object)
ENGLISH EQUIVALENTS	Expressions such as "the red one," "somebody"

It is said that human beings are efficient by nature. That efficiency is found in virtually all uses of pronouns: A pronoun replaces an understood noun, and use of a pronoun for an understood noun lightens the load, so to speak.

> *I see Daisy, Lily, and Kitty.*
> *I see **them**.*

Qualitative adjective pronouns

In Spanish, this same efficiency is seen when descriptive, or *qualitative*, adjectives become pronouns. In English, we generally add the word "one," as in the sentence "He has the green apple, and I have the red one." In Spanish, the adjective assumes the entire meaning of the noun: **Él tiene la manzana verde y yo tengo la roja.** The adjective retains the gender and number of the omitted noun, as well as the appropriate definite article (**el**, **la**, **los**, or **las**). In the sentence, it also represents the full meaning of the noun.

Él lee el libro grande, y yo leo **el pequeño**.	*He reads the big book, and I read **the small one**.*
A mí me gusta la mesa azul, pero a ti te gusta **la roja**.	*I like the blue table, but you like **the red one**.*
Tú llevas zapatos negros y yo llevo **los amarillos**.	*You wear black shoes and I wear **yellow ones**.*
Nosotros pintamos las casas enormes y ellos pintan **las muy pequeñas**.	*We paint the enormous houses, and they paint **the very small ones**.*

Traducción *Unless otherwise indicated, use the second-person singular Spanish form for English* you.

1. *He buys new cars, but I always buy used ones.*

   _____

2. *She prefers tall men, but I prefer short ones.*

   _____

3. *They want the easy question, but we want the difficult one.*

   _____

4. *She thinks that the blond* (rubio) *man is handsome, but I prefer the brown-haired* (moreno) *one.*

   _____

5. *The blue pen is yours, but the green one is mine.*

   _____

6. *Almost every client* (el cliente) *wants to buy a luxury* (de lujo) *car, but he buys the compact one.*

   _____

7. *More people buy the gray carpet* (la alfombra), *because the white (one) is always dirty* (sucio).

   _____

8. *The two short dresses are beautiful, but the long* (largo) *one is more elegant.*

   _____

9. *He puts the big lamps* (la lámpara) *in the living room and the small ones in the bedroom.*

   _____

10. *The big glass* (la copa) *is for the red wine, and the small one is for the white (wine).*

    _____

Quantitative adjective pronouns

Adjectives that are quantitative tell us the number or amount of the noun to which they refer. When a number is placed before a noun (for example, "two cats"), that number functions as an adjective. When the noun is understood and dropped, the adjective takes on the status of a pronoun, because it includes the meaning of the noun. (For a review of numbers used as pronouns, see Chapter 6.)

Yo tengo tres cajas y él tiene **cuatro**.	*I have three boxes and he has **four** (boxes).*
Hay dos mesas allí, pero sólo **una** aquí.	*There are two tables there, but only **one** (table) here.*

Note that the number **uno** ("one") takes gender.

Many quantitative adjectives are not actual numbers themselves. Instead, they refer to an amount, with an indirect way of revealing number. Most of these words can function as adjectives: **algunos platos** ("some plates"), **todos los invitados** ("all the guests"). When they stand alone or are used to refer to a noun or other antecedent, they function as pronouns: **algunos** ("some of them"), **todos** ("all of them"). Below are several commonly used quantitative adjectives.

VOCABULARIO	
algunos, algunas	some (of them), any (of them)
ambos, ambas	both (of them)
cada uno, cada una	each one
demasiado, demasiada	too much
demasiados, demasiadas	too many
la mayoría	the majority (of people)
los demás, las demás	the rest (of them)
los dos, las dos	both, the two (of them)
más	more (of it, of them)
menos	less, fewer
mucho, mucha	a lot (of something)
muchos, muchas	a lot (of things), many things
nada	nothing
ninguno, ninguna	none, neither one, not anything, not a single one
otro, otra	another, the other (one)
poco, poca	(a) little
primero, primera	first
todo, toda	everything, all
último, última	last
unos, unas	some
unos cuantos, unas cuantas	a few (of them)
varios, varias	several

A él le gusta el vestido rojo más que el verde, pero a mí me gustan **ambos**.

*He likes the red dress more than the green one, but I like **both** (of them).*

Jorge come todas las galletas en el paquete, pero Felipe come sólo **unas cuantas**.

*Jorge eats all the cookies in the package, but Felipe eats only **a few** (of them).*

Cada año intento ahorrar dinero, pero acabo por gastar **demasiado**.

*Every year I try to save money, but I end up spending **too much** (of it).*

Todos los miembros querían participar en el comité, pero **ninguno** quería trabajar duro.

*All the members wanted to be on the committee, but **none** wanted to work hard.*

EJERCICIO
7·2

Traducción

1. *Some people live in the city, and some (of them) live in the country* (el campo).

_____

2. *Seventy percent* (el _____ por ciento) *of the dentists use this toothbrush* (el cepillo de dientes), *and the rest (of them) use a stick* (el palo).

_____

3. *I can't decide which is the better dishwasher* (el lavaplatos). *I like them both.*

_____

4. *I never go shopping* (ir de compras) *with her. She buys everything. It's dangerous* (peligroso).

_____

5. *Diego likes parties. He's always the last (one) to leave* (en salir).

_____

6. *My cat drinks milk all the time. Therefore* (por eso), *I buy a lot (of it) every week.*

_____

7. *I have several Spanish books. Do you want one?*

_____

8. *Esmeralda loves* (encantar) *shoes. She has lots (of them).*

_____

9. *In the meetings* (la reunión), *a few people talk all the time, and the majority (of them) suffer in silence.*

_____

10. *Marcia receives all the presents, and poor little* (pobrecita) *Jan doesn't receive a single one.*

_____

11. *We have lots of salad. Do you want more (of it)?*

_____

12. *Usually, thousands* (miles) *of people come to the ceremony, but this year, obviously* (obviamente), *there are fewer.*

_____

13. *The students are going on a field trip* (de excursión). *Each one has a backpack* (la mochila).

_____

14. *Each girl* (la chica) *has a pencil, but several (of them) don't have paper.*

_____

15. *I'm going to order* (pedir) *another milkshake* (el batido). *Do you want another (one), too?*

_____

Adjective pronouns that refer to unspecified people

When a pronoun replaces a known person, a subject pronoun is often used. Instead of "John," we use "he"; for "John and Carlos," we use "they," and so on.

Frequently, however, we speak of people whose names we do not know, cannot know, or whose identity, considering the situation, is irrelevant. In these cases, use an appropriate pronoun. Below are several common adjective pronouns that refer to unspecified people.

alguien	someone, somebody
cualesquiera	any [*pl.*]
cualquiera	anyone, anybody, any one (person)
el mayor, la mayor	the oldest (one)
el menor, la menor	the youngest (one)
el que, la que	the one who, he who, she who
los que, las que	they who, those who, the ones who
nadie	no one, nobody
ninguno, ninguna	neither one
todos, todas	everyone, everybody

El mayor recibe todos los privilegios.	**The oldest (one)** receives all the privileges.
Santa Claus tiene regalos para **todos**.	Santa Claus has gifts for **everybody**.
Alguien aquí puede preparar la cena.	**Somebody** here can make dinner.
Nadie va de compras aquí.	**No one** goes shopping here.
Cualquiera de mis amigos puede hablar español.	**Any one** of my friends can speak Spanish.
Cualesquiera de ustedes harían lo mismo.	**Any** of you would do the same thing.

EJERCICIO 7·3

Traducción

1. *Often* (a menudo) *the youngest* [m.] *wears used clothing.*

   _____

2. *Everybody thinks that this is brilliant.*

   _____

3. *Nobody is going to eat this. It's moldy* (mohoso)*!*

   _____

4. *Someone is in the kitchen with Dinah.*

   _____

5. *Our favorite customer* (la cliente), *the one who spends* (gastar) *a lot of her money on cosmetics* (los cosméticos) *and clothing, is here today.*

   _____

6. *In the books of Harry Potter, Hermione is the oldest and Harry is the youngest of the three main characters* (el personaje)*.*

   _____

7. *Those who work ten hours a day* (al día) *in these positions* (el puesto) *are well paid* (bien remunerados)*.*

   _____

8. *Many psychologists* (el psicólogo) *study the differences between the oldest (child) and the youngest (child) in the family.*

_____

9. *Oscar Wilde writes that a cynic* (el cínico) *is he who knows the price* (el precio) *of everything and the value* (el valor) *of nothing.*

_____

10. *Everyone suffers from time to time* (de vez en cuando), *and the majority are stronger for* (por) *the experience.*

_____

11. *Everybody is here, but some (of them) don't know anybody.*

_____

12. *Juan and Mateo live together, but neither (one) has a television* (el televisor).

_____

13. *Anybody can wear these pants.*

_____

14. *Ramón gives advice* (dar consejos) *to anyone.*

_____

15. *There is a party tonight. Any [pl.] of you can go with me.*

_____

Adjective pronouns that refer to unspecified things

With things, as with people, when the name of the referent is either unknown or irrelevant, you need a nonspecific, gender-neutral pronoun.

Below are several common adjective pronouns that refer to unspecified things.

VOCABULARIO	
algo	something, anything
cualesquiera	any [*pl.*]
cualquiera	anything, any one (thing), whichever, whatever
lo mejor	the best (thing)
lo mismo	the same (thing)
lo peor	the worst (thing)
nada	nothing, not anything

Puedes tener **cualquiera** de estas galletas.   *You can have **any one** of these cookies.*

Puedes responder a **cualesquiera** de estas preguntas.   *You can reply to **any** of these questions.*

Cuando vamos de vacaciones, siempre hacemos **lo mismo**.   *When we go on vacation, we always do **the same thing**.*

Lo mejor en la vida es gratis.

Tengo algo para ti.

The best in life is free. (*The best* [things in life] are free.)

I have **something** *for you.*

Traducción *Unless otherwise indicated, use the second-person singular Spanish form for English* you.

1. *Do you have anything for* (para) *me?*

_____

2. *Of all the things in the world, the best is love.*

_____

3. *It doesn't matter* (no importa) *if I wear blue jeans* (los blue-jeans). *She always wears the same (thing).*

_____

4. *Which one do they want? Whatever. It doesn't matter.*

_____

5. *It's wonderful when you* [pl., formal] *dance. The best is when you dance the mambo.*

_____

6. *The service* (el servicio) *and the ambience* (el ambiente) *here are terrible. But the worst is the food.*

_____

7. *He never brings anything to a party, but he always eats and drinks everything.*

_____

8. *The worst (thing) in a relationship* (la relación) *is to not be able to trust* (tener confianza en) *the other person.*

_____

9. *Some people think that he's very wise* (sabio), *but the truth is that he always says the same thing.*

_____

10. *I don't know anything about* (acerca de) *this.*

_____

11. *Any one of these cars is good for* (para) *the winter.*

_____

12. *These books are interesting. You can read any one of them.*

_____

Adjective Pronouns **47**

13. *Any one of these three is okay.*

_____

14. *Any [pl.] of these are okay.*

_____

Traducción

VOCABULARIO

el anuncio	*ad*
el buhonero	*huckster*
la contraportada	*back*
entregar	*to deliver*
el letrero	*sign*
la mentira	*lie*
prometer	*to promise*
el resto de	*the rest of*
suponer	*to suppose*
la verdad	*true* (lit., *truth*)
la vida	*life*

This sign says, "Today is the first day of the rest of your life." If this is true, then what is tomorrow?
The second? I can't believe everything that I read. No one can. Some (people) believe everything.
Some people believe the ads in the backs of magazines. I suppose that some of these are true,
but the majority of these ads are lies. Who are these hucksters? They promise everything and deliver
nothing.

_____

_____

_____

_____

_____

_____

Relative Pronouns

FUNCTION	To represent understood or omitted material, thereby allowing the combination of two or more clauses
SPANISH PLACEMENT	As a separator between the independent (principal) clause and the dependent clause of a sentence
ENGLISH EQUIVALENTS	"who," "whom," "which," "whichever," "what," "whatever," "that," "whose"

A relative pronoun refers to something that has been previously stated or is understood, and thus the pronoun is related to that referent. For that reason, these pronouns are called relative pronouns.

VOCABULARIO

cuyo, cuya, cuyos, cuyas	whose
el cual, la cual	the one who, the one that
el que, la que	the one who, the one that
lo que	that which, what, whatever
los cuales, las cuales	those who, those that
los que, las que	those who, those that
que	that, who, which
PREPOSICIÓN + **que**	PREPOSITION + that, PREPOSITION + which
PREPOSICIÓN + **quien(es)**	PREPOSITION + whom

Restrictive vs. nonrestrictive clauses

Before we move forward, it is necessary to understand the concepts of restrictive and nonrestrictive clauses. A grasp of these concepts will facilitate your work with relative pronouns in this chapter.

Restrictive clause

A restrictive clause contains information that is essential to the meaning of the sentence. In other words, it restricts the meaning of the word or words to which it refers. If this clause were removed, the sentence would change meaning or it would become meaningless or ridiculous.

*A lamp **that doesn't have a bulb** is useless.*

In this sentence, the dependent clause "that doesn't have a bulb" is restrictive because it is necessary to the overall meaning of the sentence. If we remove this clause, we are left with the independent clause "A lamp is useless," which is a grammatically correct sentence, but the essential meaning has changed dramatically and what remains is absurd.

Nonrestrictive clause

A nonrestrictive clause contains information that is usually helpful to the overall meaning of the sentence, but it is not essential. If a nonrestrictive clause were removed, the sentence would stand on its own.

*Cats, **which sometimes live fifteen years or longer**, make nice pets.*

The dependent clause, "which sometimes live fifteen years or longer," although informative, does not change the basic meaning of the sentence. The independent clause, "Cats make nice pets," can easily stand alone as a grammatically correct sentence that retains its original meaning. The dependent clause is not essential for us to understand the sentence, and it could be left out. Because the information contained in a nonrestrictive clause is not necessary to the overall meaning of the sentence, the nonrestrictive clause is usually set off from the main sentence by commas.

Use of **que**

The relative pronouns "that," "who," and "which" in English all translate as **que** in Spanish. Whereas English relative pronouns distinguish between living ("who") and nonliving ("that," "which") referents, there is no such distinction in Spanish in this context.

el caballo **que** gana la carrera	*the horse **that** wins the race*
los estudiantes **que** leen el capítulo	*the students **who** read the chapter*
el lago, **que** está contaminado,	*the lake, **which** is polluted,*

Note that the relative pronoun **que** sets up both restrictive and nonrestrictive clauses.

In English, the relative pronoun is sometimes omitted, so that both of the following are correct: "I have the towels you need" and "I have the towels *that* you need." In Spanish, however, the relative pronoun cannot be omitted: You must include the Spanish word **que**.

Tengo las toallas **que** necesitas.	*I have the towels you need.*
Compramos la comida **que** pides.	*We buy the food you request.*
Él es el hombre **que** escribe esto.	*He is the man **who** writes this.*
Ellos venden casas **que** cuestan mucho.	*They sell houses **that** cost a lot.*

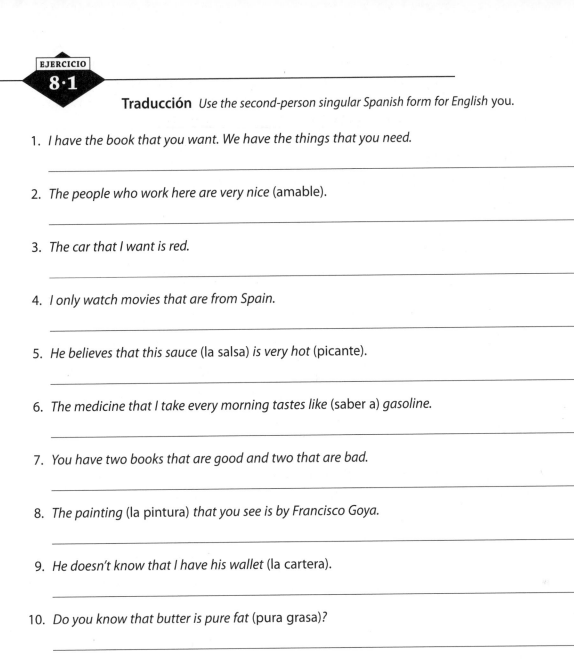

Traducción *Use the second-person singular Spanish form for English* you.

1. *I have the book that you want. We have the things that you need.*

_____

2. *The people who work here are very nice* (amable).

_____

3. *The car that I want is red.*

_____

4. *I only watch movies that are from Spain.*

_____

5. *He believes that this sauce* (la salsa) *is very hot* (picante).

_____

6. *The medicine that I take every morning tastes like* (saber a) *gasoline.*

_____

7. *You have two books that are good and two that are bad.*

_____

8. *The painting* (la pintura) *that you see is by Francisco Goya.*

_____

9. *He doesn't know that I have his wallet* (la cartera).

_____

10. *Do you know that butter is pure fat* (pura grasa)?

_____

11. *The man who lives in this house is a plumber* (el plomero).

_____

12. *They don't know what they are saying.*

_____

13. *She is the old woman* (la vieja) *who lives in a shoe.*

_____

14. *The cats that have many toes* (dedos) *live in Key West, Florida.*

_____

15. *The people who vote believe that they have a lot of power* (el poder).

_____

Use of **el cual** or **el que**

When the relative pronouns "which," "who," or "whom" introduce a nonrestrictive clause (where the information is not essential to the overall meaning of the sentence), you can use **el cual** (**la cual**, **los cuales**, **las cuales**) or **el que** (**la que**, **los que**, **las que**) instead of the simple **que**.

El cual and **el que** are interchangeable. They lend a relatively formal tone to sentences, and therefore they are used primarily in writing or in formal speech. The relative pronoun **que** is used more frequently in conversation. Using the forms **el cual** and **el que** also adds greater emphasis to the nonrestrictive clauses they introduce.

Este sofá, **el cual** es disponible en veinte colores, es muy popular este año.	*This sofa, **which** is available in twenty colors, is very popular this year.*
Tu sobrina, **la que** recibe buenas notas, quiere ser maestra.	*Your niece, **the one who** gets good grades, wants to be a teacher.*
Estos huevos, **los cuales** tienen casi un año, están muy sabrosos.	*These eggs, **which** are almost a year old, are very tasty.*
Estas langostas, **las que** son de Maryland, están muy frescas.	*These lobsters, **which** are from Maryland, are very fresh.*

EJERCICIO
8·2

Traducción

1. *His wife, who is lovely, speaks four languages* (el idioma).

   _____

2. *Their dog, which is a poodle* (el perro de lana), *barks* (ladrar) *all the time.*

   _____

3. *Our house, which is one hundred years old, is known* (conocido) *for the ghosts* (el fantasma) *that live in the attic* (el desván).

   _____

4. *My rings* (el anillo), *which are silver* (de plata), *are from Taxco, Mexico.*

   _____

5. *Our books, which are still* (todavía) *in boxes, are very valuable* (valioso).

   _____

6. *The landlord* (el casero), *who also lives in this building* (el edificio), *is a very strange* (extraño) *man.*

   _____

7. *My neighbor's* (el vecino) *children, who are noisier* (más ruidoso) *than an airport* (el aeropuerto), *are little angels* (el angelito) *in church.*

   _____

8. *The poet [f.], who is the mother of two daughters, writes every day* (todos los días) *at midnight.*

   _____

9. *The White House, which is popular with tourists, is the home* (el hogar) *of the president of the United States.*

_____

10. *These wines, which are from France, are ninety years old.*

_____

11. *This paragraph, which I have just* (acabar de) *read, makes no sense* (tener sentido).

_____

12. *This attitude* (la actitud) *of apathy* (la indiferencia), *which I cannot tolerate, is contagious* (contagioso).

_____

Use of PREPOSITION + **quien** or PREPOSITION + **que**

When the relative pronoun is the object of a preposition, usage follows the pattern PREPOSITION + **quien** when the referent is a person and PREPOSITION + **que** when the referent is inanimate. The resulting clause is a restrictive clause (that is, its information is essential to the meaning of the sentence).

The English grammar rule stating that a sentence does not end with a preposition is frequently ignored. In Spanish, however, this rule continues to be honored consistently. The English examples below reflect contemporary usage, with the preposition appearing at the end of the sentences. A sentence giving the Spanish syntax follows in parentheses. Note that in Spanish, in all cases, the preposition appears before the verb in the second clause, not at the end of the sentence.

Él es el hombre **con quien** trabajo.	*He is the man I work **with**.* (*He is the man **with whom** I work.*)
Éste es el libro **en que** pienso.	*This is the book that I'm thinking **about**.* (*This is the book **about which** I'm thinking.*)
Juana es la mujer **a quien** envío la comida.	*Juana is the woman I'm sending the food **to**.* (*Juana is the woman **to whom** I'm sending the food.*)
Paco Ortiz es el hombre **por quien** voy a votar.	*Paco Ortiz is the man I'm going to vote **for**.* (*Paco Ortiz is the man **for whom** I'm going to vote.*)

Note, however, that the Spanish word **a** is not always a preposition when it appears before Spanish **quien**. In the sentences below, it is the personal **a**, not the preposition **a** ("to"), that precedes the pronouns **quien** and **quienes**.

Antonio es el hombre **a quien** amo.	*Antonio is the man I love. (Antonio is the man **whom** I love.)*
Iris y Carmen son las chicas **a quienes** conozco.	*Iris and Carmen are the girls I know. (Iris and Carmen are the girls **whom** I know.)*

Traducción *Use the second-person singular Spanish form for English you.*
The Spanish syntax is given in parentheses after the sentence to be translated.

1. *Kitty is the woman I live with. (Kitty is the woman with whom I live.)*

   _____

2. *Who is the man you live with? (Who is the man with whom you live?)*

   _____

3. *These are the people he works for (para). (These are the people for whom he works.)*

   _____

4. *The man on the left is the person I date (salir con). (The man on the left is the person with whom I go out [date].)*

   _____

5. *Margo is the woman I work for. (Margo is the woman for whom I work.)*

   _____

6. *Francisco is the man I'm thinking about (pensar en). (Francisco is the man about whom I'm thinking.)*

   _____

7. *Kim is the woman Roberto and Jesse are angry with (estar enojado/enojada con). (Kim is the woman with whom Roberto and Jesse are angry.)*

   _____

8. *Bárbara is the person I sympathize with (tener compasión por). (Bárbara is the person with whom I sympathize.)*

   _____

9. *Ana is the woman I see.*

   _____

10. *Those men are the players I watch.*

    _____

Use of **lo que**

Lo que, meaning "that which," "what," or "whatever," is a neuter relative pronoun that allows you to refer to a great abstraction, as in the sentence "You can have *whatever* you want." **Lo que** can also encompass the entirety of something that is said or done, as in the sentence "*What* you are doing is a sin."

Note that when **lo que** is used to mean "whatever," it often stands for something that is unknown or doubtful. In these cases, it is followed by a verb in the subjunctive: **Haz *lo que puedas*** ("Do *whatever you can*").

Lo que dices es interesante.	***What*** you're saying is interesting.
Él siempre hace **lo que** quiera.	He always does ***whatever*** he wants. OR
	He always does ***whatever*** he may want.
¿Tienen **lo que** necesito?	Do they have ***what*** I need?
Lo que quieres no existe.	***What*** you want doesn't exist.

EJERCICIO
8·4

Traducción *In each sentence, the word in **bold italic** translates as Spanish **lo que**. Use the second-person singular Spanish form for English* you.

1. *He never remembers (recordar) **what** I want.*

   _____

2. *She always eats **what** I eat.*

   _____

3. *On your birthday, you can ask for (pedir) **whatever** you (may) want.*

   _____

4. ***Whatever** he says is always a lie* (la mentira).

   _____

5. *Do you hear **what** I hear? Do you know **what** I know?*

   _____

6. *He doesn't understand (comprender) **what** he reads.*

   _____

7. *Some people always do **what** they shouldn't do. They are sociopaths* (el sociópata).

   _____

8. *Do you know **what** you want to do this weekend?*

   _____

9. *She eats exactly **what** is bad for (para) her, and that is why she is always sick.*

   _____

10. ***What** you need is a hug* (el abrazo).

    _____

Use of **cuyo, cuya, cuyos, cuyas**

The relative pronoun **cuyo**, meaning "whose," links the owner and the object owned. In the sentence "Peter, whose thesis is brilliant, is a fascinating man," the owner is "Peter" and "thesis" is the object owned. The word "whose" begins the dependent clause and modifies the object owned. In Spanish, the relative pronoun in this dependent clause (**cuyo, cuya, cuyos, cuyas**) must agree with the noun that immediately follows it—the object owned.

The relative pronouns **cuyo, cuya, cuyos,** and **cuyas** usually introduce a nonrestrictive clause, which is separated by commas from the main clause of the sentence.

Pedro, **cuya tesis** es brillante, es un hombre fascinante.	*Pedro, **whose thesis** is brilliant, is a fascinating man.*
Jean, **cuyo padre** es de París, habla francés.	*Jean, **whose father** is from Paris, speaks French.*
George, **cuyos abuelos** son músicos profesionales, toca bien el piano.	*George, **whose grandparents** are professional musicians, plays the piano well.*
Laura, **cuyas alfombras** tienen manchas, está muy enojada.	*Laura, **whose rugs** have stains, is very angry.*

EJERCICIO 8·5

Traducción *Unless otherwise indicated, use the second-person singular Spanish form for English you.*

1. *Marcos, whose mother is a dentist, wants to sell candy* (los dulces).

   _____

2. *The boy* (el chico), *whose book you have, is my cousin.*

   _____

3. *The actor, whose movies are terrible, is very rich.*

   _____

4. *The dentist, whose office* (el consultorio) *is in the city, lives in the suburbs* (las afueras).

   _____

5. *The children, whose parents speak only English, study Spanish.*

   _____

6. *He is the man whose dog always steals* (robar) *our newspaper.*

   _____

7. *Are you* [sing., formal] *the woman whose tree is so* (tan) *beautiful?*

   _____

8. *Are they the children whose father is the senator* (el senador) *from Colorado?*

   _____

9. *The student, whose teacher* [f.] *is from Ecuador, wants to go to Quito this summer.*

   _____

10. *Old Mrs. Hubbard, whose cupboards* (el gabinete) *are bare* (vacío), *wants to give her dog a bone* (el hueso).

_____

11. *Mark, whose father is president of a bank, cannot add* (sumar).

_____

12. *Lilia, whose store is very popular, is my best friend.*

_____

Complete each sentence with one of the following relative pronouns: **que, lo que, la que, los que, las que, cuyo, cuya, cuyos, cuyas,** PREPOSITION + **que,** PREPOSITION + **quien(es),** *or* PERSONAL **a** + **quien(es).**

1. El libro _____ yo tengo es muy interesante.

2. Tú no tienes _____ necesitamos.

3. Las personas _____ viven en casas de cristal no deben tirar piedras.

4. Pedro, _____ coche está descompuesto, tiene que tomar el autobús.

5. Él es el hombre _____ yo estimo mucho.

6. Ellas son las compañeras _____ trabajo.

7. La mujer, _____ cara puedes ver en esta foto, es una espía internacional.

8. ¡_____ él dice es basura! ¡No sabe nada!

9. Casi todo el mundo cree _____ es necesario tener electricidad en la casa.

10. Mi canción favorita de Navidad se llama "¿Oyes _____ yo oigo?"

11. En Noche Vieja (*New Year's Eve*), siempre hacemos _____ nos da la gana.

12. Hay muchas personas _____ hablan más de un idioma.

13. Mateo es el hombre _____ yo conozco bien.

14. Creo que tengo exactamente _____ ellos desean.

15. Este hombre, _____ corazón está roto, es un hombre trágico.

Traducción

VOCABULARIO		
	algo	*somewhat*
	alquilar	*to rent*
	el área [*f.*]	*area*
	el bar	*bar*
	el barco	*boat*
	el calor	*warmth*
	el centro	*downtown*
	el club	*health club*
	cualquier	*any*
	el desierto	*desert*
	la diversión	*fun*
	el guía	*guide*
	ir de pesca	*to fish*
	lo que quiera	*whatever you want*
	el lugar	*place*
	para la pesca	*for fishing*
	la piscina	*swimming pool*
	principalmente	*mostly*
	la punta	*tip*
	el resorte	*resort*
	la soledad	*privacy*
	sureño, sureña	*southern*
	la tienda	*shop*
	tranquilo, tranquila	*tranquil*
	las vacaciones	*vacation*

Cabo San Lucas, which is on the southern tip of Baja California, is a wonderful place for a tranquil vacation. The area, which is mostly in the desert, has many elegant resorts that have swimming pools, restaurants, bars, shops, and health clubs. For the most part (En su mayor parte), *you [sing., formal] can do whatever you want in the privacy of your hotel room. There is a downtown, which is somewhat small, that has a marina, which has many boats for fishing. Tourists who want to fish can rent a boat with a guide. Any person whose idea of fun is warmth and sun can be very content for a week in Cabo San Lucas.*

_____

_____

_____

_____

_____

_____

_____

_____

Direct Object Pronouns

FUNCTION	To replace a noun that names the direct object of the verb in a sentence or clause
SPANISH PLACEMENT	Immediately before the conjugated verb OR attached directly to the infinitive
ENGLISH EQUIVALENTS	"me," "you," "him," "her," "it," "us," "them"

The direct object answers the question "What?" or "Whom?" with regard to the verb in a sentence or clause. Consider the sentence, "John has the book." One can ask, "*What* does John have?" "John has *the book*"; thus, "the book" is the direct object. The direct object pronoun "it" can therefore replace the direct object noun in the sentence: "John has *it*."

In the sentence, "John sees Mary," one can ask, "*Whom* does John see?" "John sees *Mary*"; thus, "Mary" is the direct object. The direct object pronoun "her" can replace "Mary" in the sentence: "John sees *her*."

SINGULAR		PLURAL	
me	*me*	nos	*us*
te	*you*	os	*you*
lo	*him, you, it*	los	*them, you*
la	*her, you, it*	las	*them, you*

Pronoun placement in affirmative sentences

In an affirmative statement or clause with one verb, the direct object pronoun immediately precedes the conjugated verb.

Yo **te** conozco.	*I know **you**.*
Lo vemos.	*We see **him**.* OR *We see **it**.*
Tú **me** amas.	*You love **me**.*
La tenéis.	*You have **it**.*
Ella **los** compra.	*She buys **them**.*
Ustedes **lo** quieren.	*You want **it**.*
Ellos **os** ven.	*They see **you**.*
Tú **nos** amas.	*You love **us**.*

Complete each sentence with the correct direct object pronoun.

1. Juan tiene el libro.   Juan _____ tiene.

2. Ellos ven a María.   Ellos _____ ven.

3. Yo conozco a Jorge y a Felipe.   Yo _____ conozco.

4. Juanita conoce España.   Juanita _____ conoce.

5. Tú lavas la ropa.   Tú _____ lavas.

6. Tú compras los huevos.   Tú _____ compras.

7. Ustedes beben la leche.   Ustedes _____ beben.

8. Yo no veo los unicornios.   Yo no _____ veo.

9. Ellas tienen el dinero.   Ellas _____ tienen.

10. Vosotros comprendéis el ejercicio. Vosotros _____ comprendéis.

11. Marta lleva el vestido a la fiesta. Marta _____ lleva a la fiesta.

12. Yo uso el portatíl cada día.   Yo _____ uso cada día.

13. Alejandro vende los zapatos.   Alejandro _____ vende.

14. Ella toma las vitaminas.   Ella _____ toma.

15. Nosotros miramos la televisión. Nosotros _____ miramos.

Traducción

1. *I love you.* _____

2. *I love him.* _____

3. *He loves me.* _____

4. *I see you* [sing., informal]. _____

5. *I know you* [sing., formal]. _____

6. *She sees him.* _____

7. *I drink it* [m.]. _____

8. *I have it* [f.]. _____

9. *You* [sing., informal] *have it* [m.]. _____

10. *She has them* [m.]. _____

11. *You love me.* _____

12. *I hate (odiar) it.* _____

13. *They love us.* _____

14. *You* [sing., informal] *see me.* _____

15. *You* [pl., informal] *know me.* _____

16. *We see her.* _____

17. *They eat it* [f.]. _____

18. *I want it* [m.]. _____

19. *We want it* [f.]. _____

20. *We have them* [f.]. _____

Respond to each of the following questions with a complete sentence, using a direct object pronoun. Respond to items 4 through 14 in the affirmative.

1. ¿Dónde compras la ropa? _____

2. ¿Dónde compras los libros? _____

3. ¿Dónde estudias español? _____

4. ¿Conoces al presidente de los Estados Unidos? _____

5. ¿Tomas un café cada día? _____

6. ¿Comprendes esta lección? _____

7. ¿Lees la revista *¡Hola!*? _____

8. ¿Lees el periódico cada día? _____

9. ¿Haces la cama cada día? _____

10. ¿Conoces la capital de España? _____

11. ¿Ves las estrellas ahora? _____

12. ¿Comes mucho pan? _____

13. ¿Miras las telenovelas (*soap operas*)? _____

14. ¿Lees poemas románticos a menudo? _____

Pronoun placement in negative sentences

In a negative sentence or clause with one verb, the direct object pronoun is placed between the word "no" (or other term of negation) and the conjugated verb.

Yo **no lo** sé.	*I **don't** know **it**.*
No lo conocemos.	*We **don't** know **him**.*
No los compras.	*You **don't** buy **them**.*
Nunca lo estudiáis.	*You **never** study **it**.*
Él **no nos** ve **jamás**.	*He **never** sees **us**.*
Ellos **no me** odian.	*They **don't** hate **me**.*

EJERCICIO
9·4

Traducción *Unless otherwise indicated, use the second-person singular Spanish form for English* you.

1. *I don't have it* [m.]. _____

2. *I don't want it* [f.]. _____

3. *I don't know him.* _____

4. *You don't know me.* _____

5. *They don't buy it* [f.]. _____

6. *He doesn't write it* [m.]. _____

7. *They don't read them* [m.]. _____

8. *She doesn't earn it* [m.]. _____

9. *I don't wear it* [m.]. _____

10. *We don't see you.* _____

11. *You don't have it* [f.]. _____

12. *They don't see it* [m.]. _____

13. *He doesn't know me.* _____

14. *They don't know us.* _____

15. *We don't use it* [m.]. _____

16. *She doesn't read it* [m.]. _____

17. *We don't sing them* [f.]. _____

18. *You* [pl., formal] *don't have it* [m.]. _____

19. *You never wear them* [m.]. _____

20. *You never see us.* _____

Pronoun placement in affirmative sentences with two verbs

In a statement or clause that contains two verbs, the first verb is conjugated and the second one remains in the infinitive form. There are two options for placement of the direct object pronoun in Spanish.

1. Place the direct object pronoun immediately before the first verb, which is conjugated.
2. Attach the direct object pronoun directly to the second verb, which is the infinitive form of the verb.

Note that both options are used in writing and in conversation; however, the second option is used more frequently.

Te quiero **ver.** Quiero **verte.**	*I want **to see you.***
Lo queremos **comprar.** Queremos **comprarlo.**	*We want **to buy it.***
Lo puedes **beber.** Puedes **beberlo.**	*You can **drink it.***
La podéis **comer.** Podéis **comerla.**	*You can **eat it.***
Él **nos** debe **visitar.** Él debe **visitarnos.**	*He should **visit us.***
Ellos **lo** deben **ver.** Ellos deben **verlo.**	*They should **see it.***

EJERCICIO 9·5

Complete each sentence with the correct direct object pronoun attached to the infinitive.

1. Yo necesito lavar la ropa. Yo necesito _____.
2. Tú quieres comer la paella. Tú quieres _____.
3. Ella tiene que escribir el informe. Ella tiene que _____.
4. Debemos limpiar la casa. Debemos _____.
5. El pianista puede tocar las canciones. El pianista puede _____.
6. Ellos pueden bailar el tango. Ellos pueden _____.
7. Quiero construir los edificios aquí. Quiero _____ aquí.
8. El gato puede ver el ratón (*mouse*). El gato puede _____.
9. Ella quiere conocer a tu madre. Ella quiere _____.
10. Prefiero oír la verdad. Prefiero _____.
11. El profesor quiere ver a tu padre ahora. El profesor quiere _____ ahora.
12. La cocinera va a preparar las tortillas. La cocinera va a _____.

13. Nadie puede oír la música ahora.   Nadie puede _____ ahora.

14. Ellos quieren conocer a mis hermanos.   Ellos quieren _____.

15. Queremos visitar el museo.   Queremos _____.

Traducción *Translate each sentence into Spanish, making changes for the direct objects as follows: For items 1 through 5, place the direct object pronoun before the conjugated verb; for items 6 through 10, attach the direct object pronoun to the infinitive.*

1. *He wants to see me.* _____

2. *She wants to kiss him.* _____

3. *You* [sing., informal] *should eat them* [m.]. _____

4. *They have to do it* [f.]. _____

5. *We want to meet them* [f.]. _____

6. *She has to sing it* [f.]. _____

7. *I should read it* [m.]. _____

8. *I want to see you* [sing., informal] *tomorrow.*

   _____

9. *They need to have it* [m.] *by* (para) *tomorrow.*

   _____

10. *Juan can see us.* _____

Pronoun placement in questions and negative sentences with two verbs

For both questions and negative statements that have two verbs, the direct object pronoun can be placed before the conjugated verb or attached directly to the infinitive, just as in affirmative sentences with two verbs.

No **lo** tengo que **leer**.
No tengo que **leerlo**. ⎬ *I don't have to **read it**.*

No **lo** queremos **hacer**.
No queremos **hacerlo**. ⎬ *We don't want **to do it**.*

¿**Lo** tienes que **estudiar** conmigo?
¿Tienes que **estudiarlo** conmigo? ⎬ *Do you have to **study it** with me?*

¿**Lo** podéis **soportar?**
¿Podéis **soportarlo?** }   *Can you (all) **stand it?***

¿Piensan en **venderlo?**   *Are you (all) thinking of **selling it?***

Usted **no** debe **ponerlo** aquí.   *You should**n't put it** here.*

EJERCICIO
9·7

Traducción *Translate each sentence into Spanish, attaching the direct object pronoun to the infinitive form. Unless otherwise indicated, use the second-person singular Spanish form for English* you.

1. *Do you want to see it [f.] with me?*

   _____

2. *Are you going to eat it [m.]?*

   _____

3. *Should we drink it [f.] now, or should we put it in the refrigerator?*

   _____

4. *Can we eat it [m.], or should we throw it into (a) the garbage?*

   _____

5. *You shouldn't put them [m.] in the living room.*

   _____

6. *If you don't want to have it [f.], you should put it in the box and return (devolver) it.*

   _____

7. *I can't wear them [m.] to a formal party.*

   _____

8. *Why can't you see me?*

   _____

9. *You don't have to do it [m.] today.*

   _____

10. *Do you want to open them [f.] in the morning and close them in the evening?*

    _____

Traducción *Translate each sentence into Spanish, placing the direct object pronoun before the conjugated verb. Unless otherwise indicated, use the second-person singular Spanish form for English* you.

1. *I don't want to see you* [m., pl., formal] *tonight.*

   _____

2. *You shouldn't return* (devolver) *it* [f.].

   _____

3. *Why can't you say it* [m.]?

   _____

4. *We are not going to see her at* (en) *the library.*

   _____

5. *She can't throw them* [f.] *in* (a) *the garbage. She should recycle* (reciclar) *them.*

   _____

6. *When can I see them* [f.]?

   _____

7. *If you don't want to hear it* [m.], *you can turn off* (apagar) *the radio.*

   _____

8. *Where do you want to store* (guardar) *them* [m.]? *Can we put them here?*

   _____

9. *Are you* [pl., formal] *going to sell it* [f.]?

   _____

10. *No, you cannot hit* (golpear) *him!*

    _____

Traducción

VOCABULARIO

en la parte inferior de la página	*at the bottom*
el contrato	*contract*
el edificio	*building*
día tras día	*day after day*
la firma	*the signature*
mantener su palabra	*to keep one's word*
los muebles	*furniture*
prometer	*to promise*
son de oro	*they're (made of) gold*
una vez más	*once again*

I know that Donald has my money, my building, and the furniture inside the building. He thinks that I don't know this, but, yes, I know it. Donald thinks that he is smarter than everyone, but he isn't. First, the money: I know that he has it because I have a document that says he owes it to me. It is a contract and it has his signature at the bottom. Second, the building: it's mine. Again, I have a contract with his signature at the bottom in which he promises it to me. Day after day, I receive nothing. He never keeps his word. Third, the furniture: once again, I know that he has my furniture because there are photos of his living room in a magazine, and it's filled with my sofa, my chairs, my tables, and more. I know this because they're gold. He believes that everything is his, but it's not true. These things are mine and I know it. And I want them now.

_____

_____

_____

_____

_____

_____

_____

_____

_____

_____

Indirect Object Pronouns

FUNCTION
To replace a noun that names the indirect object of the verb in a sentence or clause

SPANISH PLACEMENT
Immediately before the conjugated verb OR attached directly to the infinitive

ENGLISH EQUIVALENTS
"me," "you," "him," "her," "us," "them"

The indirect object answers the questions "To whom?" and "For whom?" with regard to the verb in a sentence or clause. In other words, the indirect object tells where the direct object is going.

Consider the sentence, "I give you the gift" (OR "I give the gift *to* you"). The direct object is "the gift," because this answers the question "*What* do I give?" The indirect object, then, is "you" because I am giving the gift "*to you*." "You" is where the gift is going.

In the sentence "He buys me flowers" (OR "He buys flowers *for* me"), the direct object is "flowers" (because that is *what* he buys), and the indirect object is "me" (because I am the one *for whom* he buys the flowers).

Indirect object pronouns in Spanish are as follows:

SINGULAR		PLURAL	
me	*me*	nos	*us*
te	*you*	os	*you*
le	*him, her, you*	les	*them, you*

In a sentence with an indirect object, there is always a direct object, either stated or implied. In the sentence "My grandmother writes me every week," "me" is the indirect object, because my grandmother is writing *something* (a note, a letter, a postcard, an e-mail, a text) *to me.* The direct object is understood.

EJERCICIO 10·1

In the following sentences, identify the direct and indirect objects and write each object (in English) on the appropriate line, including those cases where the direct object is understood.

	DIRECT OBJECT	INDIRECT OBJECT
1. *John tells me a lie.*		
2. *She buys him nothing.*		
3. *They send us food.*		
4. *The chef cooks us a meal.*		
5. *The cannibal cooks us for his friends.*		
6. *He tells you.*		
7. *I bought you a ring.*		
8. *He buys drinks for everyone.*		
9. *You write me every week.*		
10. *They sold the diamonds to her.*		

Pronoun placement in affirmative sentences

In Spanish, in an affirmative statement or clause with one verb, the indirect object pronoun immediately precedes the conjugated verb.

In English, however, there are two possibilities for placement of the indirect object pronoun in sentences with one verb: (1) between the verb and the direct object, or (2) in a prepositional phrase following the direct object.

Juan **me** compra un libro.	*John buys **me** a book.* / *John buys a book **for me**.*
Ella **nos** dijo una mentira.	*She told **us** a lie.* / *She told a lie **to us**.*
Yo **te** digo la verdad siempre.	*I always tell **you** the truth.* / *I always tell the truth **to you**.*
Os damos el dinero.	*We give **you** the money.* / *We give the money **to you**.*
Ella **le** escribe una carta.	*She writes **him** a letter.* / *She writes a letter **to him**.*
Él **les** canta una canción.	*He sings **them** a song.* / *He sings a song **to them**.*

Complete each sentence with the appropriate indirect object pronoun.

1. Jorge compra flores para mí.   Jorge _____ compra flores.

2. Marta cuenta la historia a nosotros.   Marta _____ cuenta la historia.

3. Los padres leen el libro al niño.   Los padres _____ leen el libro.

4. Escribo una carta a mis abuelos.   _____ escribo una carta.

5. Felipe da un anillo a Juana.   Felipe _____ da un anillo.

6. Vendemos la casa a Marta.   _____ vendemos la casa.

7. Traigo el maquillaje (*makeup*) a Mary Kay.   _____ traigo el maquillaje.

8. Preparamos la cena para Guillermo.   _____ preparamos la cena.

9. Compras la falda para mí.   _____ compras la falda.

10. Daisy planta un árbol para nosotros.   Daisy _____ planta un árbol.

11. Ella escribe una carta a ustedes.   Ella _____ escribe una carta.

12. Enviamos el regalo a vosotros.   _____ enviamos el regalo.

13. Sirvo la comida a ellas.   _____ sirvo la comida.

14. El arquitecto diseña una casa para ti.   El arquitecto _____ diseña una casa.

15. El mesero sirve la bebida a Isabel.   El mesero _____ sirve la bebida.

Traducción

1. *I tell him the truth.*

_____

2. *He doesn't tell me the truth. He tells me a lie* (la mentira).

_____

3. *We give her the flowers, and she gives us the money.*

_____

4. *I write them a letter every week.*

_____

5. *They write to us every month.*

_____

6. *She sings him a song.*

_____

7. *John is my assistant* (el ayudante), *and I tell him everything.*

_____

8. *I always tell her that she's pretty.*

_____

9. *I send them a card* (la tarjeta) *for their anniversary.*

_____

10. *What do they give you* [sing., informal] *for your birthday every year?*

_____

Pronoun placement in negative sentences

In a negative statement or clause with one verb, the indirect object pronoun is placed between the word "no" (or other term of negation) and the conjugated verb.

Él **no me** trae nada.	He does**n't** bring **me** anything.
Ellos **no nos** dicen la verdad.	They do**n't** tell **us** the truth.
La médica **no te** da medicina.	The doctor does**n't** give **you** medicine.
Nunca os damos regalos.	We **never** give **you** gifts.
No le envío la cuenta **jamás.**	I **never** send **him** the bill.
No les vendes el pan.	You do**n't** sell **them** the bread.

EJERCICIO
10·4

Traducción *Unless otherwise indicated, use the second-person singular Spanish form for English* you.

1. *He doesn't tell me anything.*

_____

2. *I don't tell him anything.*

_____

3. *They never send him anything because they don't know his address.*

_____

4. *I don't give her money because she never says (to me) "thank you."*

_____

5. *The waiter doesn't sing "Happy Birthday" to you.*

_____

6. *Why don't they tell her the truth?*

_____

7. *Why don't they buy you* [pl., informal] *a new laptop?*

_____

8. *I serve them dinner, but they never thank* (dar las gracias) *me. How rude!* (¡Qué grosero!)

_____

9. *If you* [pl., formal] *don't ask me questions* (hacer preguntas), *I don't tell you lies.*

_____

10. *We don't lend* (prestar) *them money.*

_____

Pronoun placement in affirmative sentences with two verbs

In a statement or clause that contains two verbs, the first verb is conjugated and the second one remains in the infinitive form. In Spanish, there are two options for placement of the indirect object pronoun:

1. Place the indirect object pronoun immediately before the first verb, which is conjugated.
2. Attach the indirect object pronoun directly to the second verb, which is the infinitive form of the verb.

Note that both options are used in writing and in conversation; however, the second option is used more frequently.

Él **me** quiere **dar** un regalo. Él quiere **darme** un regalo.	*He wants **to give me** a gift.*
Tú **nos** necesitas **comprar** algo. Tú necesitas **comprarnos** algo.	*You need **to buy us** something.*
Te puedo **decir** todo. Puedo **decirte** todo.	*I can **tell you** everything.*
Os preferimos **prestar** el dinero. Preferimos **prestaros** el dinero.	*We prefer **to lend you** the money.*
Él **le** quiere **vender** el coche. Él quiere **venderle** el coche.	*He wants **to sell her** the car.*
Ella **les** debe **alquilar** la casa. Ella debe **alquilarles** la casa.	*She should **rent** the house **to them**.*

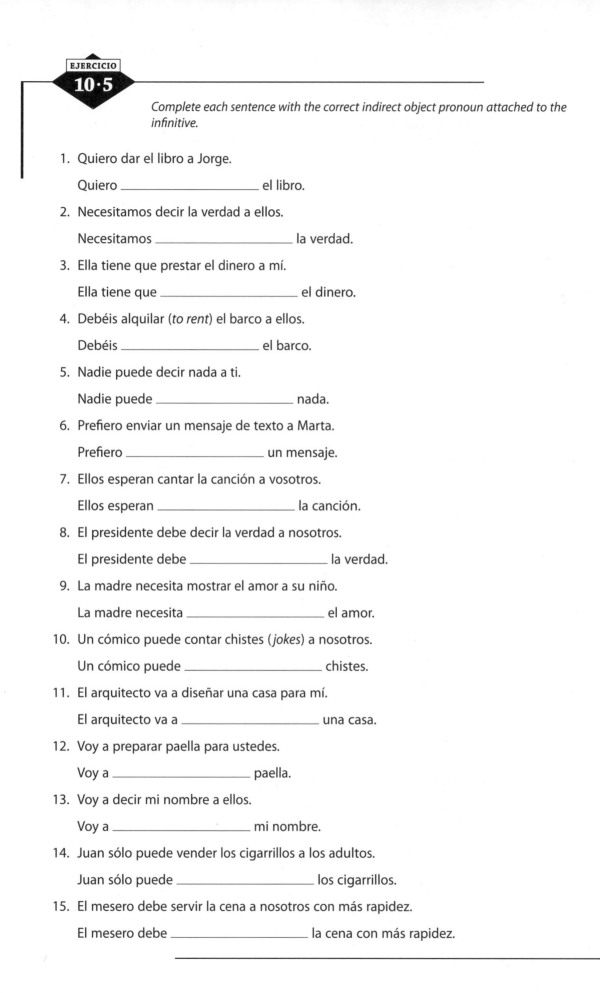

EJERCICIO

10·5

Complete each sentence with the correct indirect object pronoun attached to the infinitive.

1. Quiero dar el libro a Jorge.

   Quiero _____ el libro.

2. Necesitamos decir la verdad a ellos.

   Necesitamos _____ la verdad.

3. Ella tiene que prestar el dinero a mí.

   Ella tiene que _____ el dinero.

4. Debéis alquilar (*to rent*) el barco a ellos.

   Debéis _____ el barco.

5. Nadie puede decir nada a ti.

   Nadie puede _____ nada.

6. Prefiero enviar un mensaje de texto a Marta.

   Prefiero _____ un mensaje.

7. Ellos esperan cantar la canción a vosotros.

   Ellos esperan _____ la canción.

8. El presidente debe decir la verdad a nosotros.

   El presidente debe _____ la verdad.

9. La madre necesita mostrar el amor a su niño.

   La madre necesita _____ el amor.

10. Un cómico puede contar chistes (*jokes*) a nosotros.

    Un cómico puede _____ chistes.

11. El arquitecto va a diseñar una casa para mí.

    El arquitecto va a _____ una casa.

12. Voy a preparar paella para ustedes.

    Voy a _____ paella.

13. Voy a decir mi nombre a ellos.

    Voy a _____ mi nombre.

14. Juan sólo puede vender los cigarrillos a los adultos.

    Juan sólo puede _____ los cigarrillos.

15. El mesero debe servir la cena a nosotros con más rapidez.

    El mesero debe _____ la cena con más rapidez.

Traducción *Translate each of the following sentences into Spanish, making changes to the indirect objects as follows: For items 1 through 5, place the indirect object pronoun before the conjugated verb. For items 6 through 10, attach the indirect object pronoun to the infinitive.*

1. *I want to give him a gift.*

   _____

2. *He needs to tell me the truth.*

   _____

3. *We should write her a letter.*

   _____

4. *You* [sing., informal] *should write to us more often* (más a menudo).

   _____

5. *You* [pl., formal] *have to tell them the truth.*

   _____

6. *We should give them olive oil* (el aceite de oliva).

   _____

7. *He wants to buy her a diamond* (el diamante).

   _____

8. *When he comes to our house, he always wants to bring* (traer) *us something.*

   _____

9. *I can't send you* [sing., informal] *these vases* (el florero) *through the mail* (por correo).

   _____

10. *You* [pl., informal] *need to tell him something.*

    _____

Pronoun placement in questions and negative sentences with two verbs

In Spanish questions and negative statements with two verbs, the indirect object pronoun can be placed before the conjugated verb or attached directly to the infinitive.

¿Quién **me** va a **enviar** una cuenta? ¿Quién va a **enviarme** una cuenta?	*Who is going **to send me** a bill?*
Él **no nos** necesita **dar** la información. Él **no** necesita **darnos** la información.	*He doesn't need **to give us** the information.*

¿**Te** debemos **decir** la verdad?   }   *Should we **tell you** the truth?*
¿Debemos **decirte** la verdad?

No os quiero **vender** estos collares.   }   *I don't want **to sell you** these necklaces.*
No quiero **venderos** estos collares.

Nunca le podéis **comprar** la felicidad.   }   *You (all) can **never buy** happiness **for her**.*
Nunca podéis **comprarle** la felicidad.

No les tengo que **decir** nada.   }   *I don't have **to tell them** anything.*
No tengo que **decirles** nada.

Respond to each statement or question with two separate sentences in order to show both options for the placement of the indirect object pronoun. Unless otherwise indicated, use the second-person singular Spanish form for English you.

1. *Do you want to bring me a kitten?*

_____

_____

2. *We're not going to show them our latest findings* (los últimos hallazgos).

_____

_____

3. *Do you want to sell them these paintings?*

_____

_____

4. *Who is going to pay me the money?*

_____

_____

5. *Can you send the furniture* (los muebles) *to us by* (para) *Tuesday?*

_____

_____

6. *The artist can't paint her a picture* (el cuadro) *by June.*

_____

_____

7. *I'm not going to wash your clothing for you.*

_____

_____

8. *We don't want to tell you* [pl., formal] *the bad news* (las malas noticias).

_____

_____

9. *When can you* [pl., informal] *build* (construir) *the building* (el edificio) *for us?*

_____

_____

10. *Should you write her such a letter* (tal carta)?

_____

_____

Redundant use of indirect object pronouns

The principal purpose of any pronoun is to *replace* a noun. However, there are times when it is clearer or more emphatic to use *both* the pronoun and **a** + NOUN or **a** + PRONOUN. When this occurs with the indirect object pronoun, it is usually in third-person situations.

Below is a list of verbs that frequently take both the pronoun and the **a** + NOUN or **a** + PRONOUN construction.

VOCABULARIO			
comprar	to buy	**mandar**	to send
dar	to give	**pedir**	to ask (*a favor*), request (from)
decir	to say, tell	**preguntar**	to ask (*a question*)
escribir	to write	**preparar**	to prepare
enviar	to send	**regalar**	to give a gift
hacer	to make, do	**traer**	to bring

Yo **le** doy **a Juan** cinco dólares.	*I give **John** five dollars.*
Manuel **les** escribe **a sus padres** cada semana.	*Manuel writes to **his parents** every week.*
Les pregunto **a ellos** si quieren ir.	*I ask **them** if they want to go.*
Le pido **a mi jefe** un aumento.	*I ask **my boss** for a raise.*

Note that in the preceding examples, the addition of **a** + NOUN or **a** + PRONOUN neither replaces nor adds necessary information. The two reasons to include the **a** + NOUN or **a** + PRONOUN in a sentence, clarity and emphasis, are illustrated below.

Clarity

The third-person noun or pronoun helps to clarify the ambiguous third-person pronoun **le**.

Le dije el chiste.	*I told **him?**/**her?**/**you?** the joke.*
Le dije **a Juan** el chiste.	*I told **Juan** the joke.*
Le dije el chiste **a él**.	*I told **him** the joke.*
Le dije el chiste **a usted**.	*I told **you** the joke.*
Le dije el chiste **a ella**.	*I told **her** the joke.*

Emphasis

The prepositional phrase adds emphasis to the noun or pronoun.

Juan **me** dijo **a mí** ese chiste.	*Juan told __me__ that joke.*
¿Juan **te** dijo ese chiste **a ti**?	*Juan told __you__ that joke?*
Juan **nos** dijo ese chiste **a nosotros**.	*Juan told __us__ that joke.*
Juan **les** dijo ese chiste **a ellas**.	*Juan told __them__ that joke.*

EJERCICIO
10·8

Traducción *Unless otherwise indicated, use the second-person singular Spanish form for English* you.

1. *I tell Juan everything.*

_____

2. *I want to tell him everything.*

_____

3. *She writes to her aunt every month.*

_____

4. *Why do you bring so much* (tanto) *to Mateo?*

_____

5. *She gives the documents to her attorney* (el abogado).

_____

6. *She has to give the money to the police* (la policía).

_____

7. *Margarita is giving* (regalar) *us a horse!*

_____

8. *Oliver wants to give* (regalar) *me a watch from Cartier!*

_____

9. *What are you making for* (a) *your friends? I'm making them a cake* (la torta).

_____

10. *I bring them a newspaper every morning.*

_____

11. *I usually buy them* [f.] *clothing for* (para) *Christmas.*

_____

12. *What should we buy her?*

_____

13. *Romeo sends Julieta roses on Valentine's Day.*

_____

14. *Are they going to send you* [pl., formal] *anything this year?*

_____

15. *George Washington cannot tell a lie* (la mentira) *to anyone.*

_____

Indirect object pronouns with **gustar**

There is a group of Spanish verbs that use indirect object pronouns in a construction that, to many native English speakers, seems to work in reverse. The most commonly used verb of this type is **gustar** ("to be pleasing to").

In English, one would say, "I like the bread," with "I" as the subject and "the bread" as the direct object. In Spanish, one would say, **Me gusta el pan.** This means literally "The bread is pleasing to me," with "the bread" now the subject of the sentence (instead of "I"). In this Spanish sentence, "I" has become the indirect object in the form of the Spanish **me.**

Because the meaning of the Spanish sentence is "the bread is pleasing *to me*" (since the indirect object often contains or implies the preposition *to*), the indirect object pronoun is needed. This construction is used for the verb **gustar** and other verbs that are used like **gustar.**

The verbs in this section nearly always appear in their third-person singular and plural forms. The things that are being discussed have their effect on people: "Chicago fascinates *me,*" "traffic bothers *you,*" "autobiographies interest *her,*" "gossip is not important *to him.*"

To work with **gustar** and verbs like **gustar**, use the following pattern:

INDIRECT OBJECT PRONOUN + THIRD-PERSON [*sing.* or *pl.*] VERB + NOUN

SINGULAR SUBJECT (NOUN)	PLURAL SUBJECT (NOUN)	
Me **gusta la pintura**.	Me **gustan las pinturas**.	*I like the painting/paintings.* (*The painting is liked by me. / The paintings are liked by me.*)
Te **gusta el anillo**.	Te **gustan los anillos**.	*You like the ring/rings.* (*The ring is liked by you. / The rings are liked by you.*)
Le **gusta el zorro**.	Le **gustan los zorros**.	*He/She likes the fox/foxes.* (*The fox is liked by him/her. / The foxes are liked by him/her.*) *You like the fox/foxes.* (*The fox is liked by you. / The foxes are liked by you.*)
Nos **gusta la culebra**.	Nos **gustan las culebras**.	*We like the snake/snakes.* (*The snake is liked by us. / The snakes are liked by us.*)
Os **gusta la lámpara**.	Os **gustan las lámparas**.	*You like the lamp/lamps.* (*The lamp is liked by you. / The lamps are liked by you.*)
Les **gusta el reloj**.	Les **gustan los relojes**.	*They/You like the clock/clocks.* (*The clock is liked by them/you. / The clocks are liked by them/you.*)

When working with **gustar** and verbs like **gustar**, remember the following points:

1. With the verb **gustar**, if what is liked (or is pleasing) is an action rather than a thing, substitute the infinitive of the appropriate verb for the noun.

Me gusta **correr**.	*I like **to run**.*
No me gusta ni **correr** ni **nadar**.	*I don't like **to run** or **swim**.*

2. To clarify the person being referred to in the third person, precede the clause with **a** + the person's name or **a** + PRONOUN.

A Madonna le gusta cantar.	***Madonna** likes to sing.*
A Tom Hanks le gusta estudiar la historia.	***Tom Hanks** likes to study history.*
A él le gusta dirigir películas también.	***He** also likes to direct movies.*

3. Adding the person's name or repeating a pronoun adds emphasis.

A mí me gusta el chisme.	<u>*I*</u> *like gossip.*
A ti te gustan los deportes.	<u>*You*</u> *like sports.*

4. When a noun is used in the abstract, Spanish uses the definite article, whether the referent noun is singular or plural.

A mí me gusta **el té**.	*I like **tea**.*
A él le gustan **las galletas**.	*He likes **cookies**.*

5. When what is liked (or is pleasing) is simply "it," as in the sentence "I like it," the English word "it" is not translated into Spanish. The word "it," as the subject of the Spanish sentence, is simply understood. This is also true for the plural form "them."

Me gusta.	*I like **it**.*
Me gustan.	*I like **them**.*

6. To negate a sentence of this type (for example, "I don't like . . ."), place "no" before the indirect object pronoun.

No me gusta el chisme.	*I **don't** like gossip.*
No me gusta.	*I **don't** like it.*

EJERCICIO

¿Qué piensas tú? ¿Verdadero o falso?

_____ 1. Me gusta la comida mexicana.

_____ 2. Me gustan los dibujos animados (*cartoons*) en la televisión los sábados por la mañana.

_____ 3. No me gusta cuando una persona me llama por teléfono a las tres de la mañana.

_____ 4. Al presidente de los Estados Unidos le gusta la política.

_____ 5. A Sherlock Holmes le gustan las intrigas.

_____ 6. En este país, normalmente nos gusta la democracia.

_____ 7. A muchas personas les gusta celebrar la Noche Vieja (*New Year's Eve*) en una fiesta.

_____ 8. A mí no me gusta ir de compras en una tienda muy grande.

_____ 9. A mi mejor amigo/amiga le gusta bailar en las discotecas.

_____ 10. A un abogado le gusta ganar los casos.

_____ 11. No me gusta bailar ni cantar delante de muchas personas.

_____ 12. A Donald Trump le gustan muchísimo el dinero y el poder.

EJERCICIO
10·9

Answer the following questions using **gustar**, *either affirmatively or negatively—whichever is true for you. The first item is done for you.*

1. ¿Te gusta la leche?

   Sí, me gusta la leche. OR *No, no me gusta la leche.*

2. ¿Te gustan los dramas de Shakespeare?

   _____

3. ¿Te gusta comer en el coche?

   _____

4. ¿Te gusta limpiar la casa?

   _____

5. ¿Te gustan los platos (*dishes*) exóticos?

   _____

6. ¿Te gustan las películas de horror?

   _____

7. ¿Te gusta correr?

   _____

8. ¿Te gusta memorizar los verbos españoles?

   _____

9. ¿Te gustan los mosquitos?

   _____

10. ¿Te gusta conducir en la hora punta (*rush hour*)?

    _____

Other verbs that take the indirect object pronoun

There are several Spanish verbs that are used like **gustar**—that is, they take the indirect object pronoun and demonstrate the effect that something or someone has on a person.

Below are several frequently used verbs that are used like **gustar**. In some cases, a more common way of expressing the meaning in English follows in brackets.

VOCABULARIO	
aburrir	to be boring (to/for someone)
bastar	to be enough (to/for someone)
caer bien (mal)	to like (dislike), to go well (badly) with
disgustar	to be disgusting (to someone) [to hate]
doler (o > ue)	to be painful (to someone) [to hurt, to ache]
encantar	to be enchanting (to someone) [to love (a thing)]
faltar	to be lacking/missing (to someone) [to need (a thing)]
fascinar	to be fascinating (to someone)
importar	to be important (to someone)
interesar	to be interesting (to someone)
molestar	to be bothersome (to someone) [to bother]
parecer	to seem/appear (to someone)
sobrar	to be left over or extra (to someone)
volver (o > ue) loco/loca	to be crazy (about/for someone) [more intense than **encantar**]

EJERCICIO

¿Cuál es verdadero o falso para ti?

_____ 1. Cuando me duele la cabeza, tomo una aspirina.

_____ 2. Me importa la verdad.

_____ 3. La arquitectura de Frank Lloyd Wright me fascina.

_____ 4. Los anuncios (*commercials*) en la televisión me molestan mucho y me aburren también.

_____ 5. Me disgustan las personas que gruñen (*to grumble*) todo el tiempo.

_____ 6. A un multimillonario le sobra el dinero.

_____ 7. A los actores de Hollywood les encanta ganar el Oscar.

_____ 8. Me falta el dinero para comprar un diamante de cinco quilates (*carats*).

_____ 9. A muchos jugadores de tenis les duelen los codos.

_____ 10. No me importa tener mucho dinero ni vivir en una casa lujosa.

_____ 11. No me interesan los chismes (*gossip*).

_____ 12. A mí me parece que las joyas de Tiffany's son las mejores.

_____ 13. Me vuelve loco/loca el chocolate.

_____ 14. A un elefante le bastan dos cacahuates (*peanuts*).

_____ 15. Me caen bien mis amigos.

_____ 16. Me cae mal la carne con chocolate.

Traducción *Translate the following sentences into Spanish, using the verbs from the vocabulary box on page 82. For some items, clues to the appropriate verb are given in parentheses. Unless otherwise indicated, use the second-person singular Spanish form for English* you.

1. *This book fascinates me.*

   _____

2. *I don't want anything more. I have enough food. (The food is sufficient for me.)*

   _____

3. *She loves everything.*

   _____

4. *I hate this movie. (This movie is disgusting to me.)*

   _____

5. *My eyes hurt.*

   _____

6. *Nothing is important to him and nothing interests him. How* (qué) *sad!*

   _____

7. *I'm missing a button* (el botón) *on my shirt.*

   _____

8. *We love your new house!*

   _____

9. *What's bothering you?*

   _____

10. *These magazines seem absurd* (absurdo) *to me.*

    _____

11. *After the holidays* (los días de fiesta), *they don't have (any) money left over.*

    _____

12. *He hates coffee, but I love it.*

    _____

13. *I'm crazy about this play* (la obra de teatro).

_____

14. *I don't like cookies with raisins. (Cookies with raisins don't go well with me.)*

_____

15. *She loves sports, but he hates them.*

_____

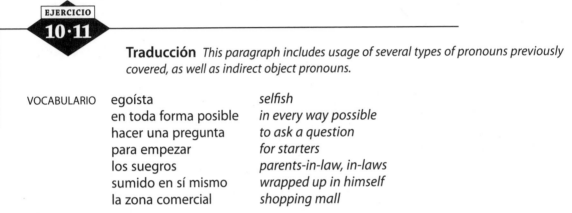

EJERCICIO

10·11

Traducción *This paragraph includes usage of several types of pronouns previously covered, as well as indirect object pronouns.*

VOCABULARIO

egoísta	*selfish*
en toda forma posible	*in every way possible*
hacer una pregunta	*to ask a question*
para empezar	*for starters*
los suegros	*parents-in-law, in-laws*
sumido en sí mismo	*wrapped up in himself*
la zona comercial	*shopping mall*

Donna's parents-in-law disgust her. They bother her in every way possible. For starters, they are boring people. They aren't interested in anything or anybody, and they have no friends because other people do not interest them. They never ask Donna or anybody a question. They bother her because they are so selfish. Her mother-in-law is fascinated by shopping malls and loves to go shopping. Her father-in-law is completely wrapped up in himself. Nothing else is important to him, except his next meal. To Donna, who has many friends and many interests, her in-laws seem to be tragic people.

_____

_____

_____

_____

_____

_____

_____

_____

Reflexive Object Pronouns

·11·

FUNCTION	To indicate that the subject and object of an action are the same person or thing
SPANISH PLACEMENT	Immediately before the conjugated verb OR attached directly to the infinitive
ENGLISH EQUIVALENTS	"myself," "yourself," "himself," "herself," "itself," "ourselves," "yourselves," "themselves"

Reflexive pronouns are tiny words that carry the power to change the meaning of a sentence.

SINGULAR		PLURAL	
me	*myself*	nos	*ourselves*
te	*yourself*	os	*yourselves*
se	*himself, herself, yourself, itself*	se	*themselves, yourselves*

The principal function of a reflexive object pronoun is to indicate that the action being performed stays with the one who performs it. If *Jane* washes *your* hair, her action has extended to you; thus, that action is not reflexive. However, when *Jane* washes *her own* hair, the action begun by Jane stays with Jane. In this case, the verb **lavarse**, meaning "to wash," is reflexive, and it requires a reflexive object pronoun.

NOT REFLEXIVE	Jane **te** lava el pelo.	*Jane washes **your** hair.*
		(lit., Jane washes the hair on/of you.)
REFLEXIVE	Jane **se** lava el pelo.	*Jane washes **her** hair.*
		(lit., Jane washes the hair on/of herself.)

Reflexive verbs in daily routines

Many of the frequently used reflexive verbs refer to the things we do routinely to prepare ourselves for the day. Below are several of the more common reflexive verbs in this category.

VOCABULARIO			
afeitarse	to shave oneself	**lavarse**	to wash oneself
bañarse	to bathe oneself	**peinarse**	to comb one's hair
cepillarse	to brush oneself	**pesarse**	to weigh oneself
ducharse	to take a shower	**secarse**	to dry oneself

Note that when a body part is mentioned, the definite article (**el**, **la**, **los**, **las**) is used to modify it rather than the possessive adjective (**mi**, **tu**, **su**, etc.). There are two reasons for this: (1) If *you* are washing the hair *on you*, it has to be *your* hair, so it is redundant to use the possessive adjective, and (2) many native Spanish speakers consider it in poor taste to mention body parts in a direct way.

In English, we generally reserve the use of the reflexive pronouns ("myself," "yourself," etc.) for what can be called "full-body experiences"—that is, "I love *myself*," "she sees *herself* in the full-length mirror," "they don't understand *themselves*." In Spanish, the use is much narrower: reflexive pronouns are used in situations that deal with a single aspect of our *selves*—for example, teeth, hair, or hands. It is a given that most of us wash our own hair (as opposed to a hair stylist washing our hair), and most of us dress ourselves and brush our own teeth, and in English we don't use the reflexive forms to express these actions. However, when an action doesn't leave the performer, in Spanish it is expressed with a reflexive verb and reflexive object pronouns.

Me lavo el pelo cada día.	*I wash my hair every day.*
Nos afeitamos dos veces al día.	*We shave twice a day.*
Te pesas cada mañana.	*You weigh yourself every morning.*
Os cepilláis los dientes.	*You brush your teeth.*
Ella **se baña** con jabón especial.	*She bathes with special soap.*
Se lavan las manos.	*They wash their hands.*

EJERCICIO
11·1

Traducción

1. *I take a shower.*

   _____

2. *I take a bath.*

   _____

3. *You* [sing., informal] *take a shower every day.*

   _____

4. *He shaves every morning.*

   _____

5. *She brushes her teeth three times a day* (al día).

   _____

6. *We brush our teeth.*

_____

7. *They shave twice a day.*

_____

8. *He washes his hair.*

_____

9. *I wash my face.*

_____

10. *You* [sing., informal] *dry your hair.*

_____

11. *You* [sing., formal] *dry yourself with a towel* (la toalla).

_____

12. *I comb my hair often* (a menudo).

_____

13. *She almost never* (casi nunca) *combs her hair.*

_____

14. *I weigh myself on the bathroom scale* (la báscula de baño).

_____

15. *She weighs herself twice a day.*

_____

What makes a verb reflexive?

It is important to note that nearly all verbs can be made reflexive. There is nothing magical about a reflexive verb. All it means is that the action is not leaving the performer. You can wash your car (not reflexive) or you can wash your face (reflexive); you can put your child to bed (not reflexive) or you can go to bed yourself/put yourself to bed (reflexive).

Because most verbs can be made reflexive, it is impossible to list all or even most of them here. Following are several verbs that are frequently used in the reflexive form because of the nature of the action they represent.

acostarse (o > ue)	to go to bed
casarse (con alguien)	to marry (someone), get married
desmayarse	to faint
despertarse (e > ie)	to wake up
desvestirse (e > i)	to get undressed
dormirse (o > ue)	to fall asleep
enfermarse	to get/become sick
enojarse	to get/become angry
hacerse	to become (*voluntarily*) (*lit.*, "to make oneself")
irse	to go away
levantarse	to stand/get up (*lit.*, "to lift oneself")
llamarse	to call oneself, to be called
mirarse	to look at oneself
ponerse	to become (*involuntarily, often emotionally*)
ponerse (la ropa)	to put on (clothing)
preocuparse (de/por/con)	to worry (about)
probarse (o > ue) (la ropa)	to try on (clothing)
quedarse	to stay, remain
quitarse (la ropa)	to take off (clothing), remove (clothing)
sentarse (e > ie)	to sit down, seat oneself
sentirse (e > ie)	to feel (*emotionally, physically*)
verse	to see oneself
vestirse (e > i)	to dress oneself

Me quedo en un hotel de lujo.	*I **stay** in a luxury hotel.*
Nos vemos en el espejo.	*We **see ourselves** in the mirror.*
Te llamas Pedro.	***Your name is*** *Pedro.* OR ***You call yourself*** *Pedro.*
Os sentáis en los sillones.	***You're sitting*** *in the easy chairs.*
Nancy **se siente** enferma.	*Nancy **feels** sick.*
Ellas **se enferman**.	*They **get sick**.*

When an item of clothing is mentioned with a reflexive verb, as in the sentence **Elisabeth se pone los zapatos** ("Elisabeth puts on her shoes"), the definite article is used to modify the noun naming the item of clothing. The reason is the same as when parts of the body are mentioned: because one can assume that a person is putting on his or her own clothes, it would be redundant to use a possessive pronoun.

EJERCICIO

¿Verdadero o falso?

_____ 1. Me enojo mucho con personas que no toman la responsabilidad por sus acciones.

_____ 2. Cuando viajo a otra ciudad, siempre me quedo en un hotel de cuatro estrellas.

_____ 3. Me levanto para cenar y me siento para caminar.

_____ 4. Si veo sangre (*blood*), me pongo enfermo/enferma y después me desmayo.

_____ 5. Cuando me enojo con alguien, hablo con esa persona para resolver el problema.

_____ 6. Es importante ponerse manoplas (*mittens*) y una chaqueta de lana (*wool*) cuando hace mucho frío.

_____ 7. Siempre me quito los zapatos antes de entrar en la casa.

_____ 8. Muchas personas se ponen muy furiosas cuando conducen en las autopistas.

_____ 9. El presidente de Bielorrusia se llama Günther.

_____ 10. Cuando una persona se casa con otra persona, esta ceremonia se llama la boda.

_____ 11. Cuando una persona se queda en un hotel de lujo, normalmente se siente muy elegante.

_____ 12. Una persona puede hacerse millonaria si trabaja quince horas al día durante veinte años.

_____ 13. Me siento triste por las personas pobres del mundo.

_____ 14. Me cepillo los dientes cada noche antes de acostarme.

_____ 15. Me levanto a las tres de la mañana.

EJERCICIO
11·2

Traducción

1. *When I try on new clothing, I look at myself in the mirror.*

   _____

2. *What time* (a qué hora) *do you* [sing., informal] *go to bed and what time do you get up?*

   _____

3. *Normally people get married on* (durante) *the weekends.*

   _____

4. *I get sick when I eat food that has a lot of fat* (la grasa).

   _____

5. *I go (away) to work* (al trabajo) *every morning at eight o'clock.*

   _____

6. *I take a shower, I brush my teeth, I dry my hair, I get dressed, and then I go to work.*

   _____

7. *I become (involuntarily) sick when I see a hair* (el pelo) *in the food.*

   _____

8. *Miss America faints when she puts on the crown* (la corona).

   _____

9. *Every night I get undressed, I put on my pajamas* (el pijama), *I go to bed, and I fall asleep.*

10. *When Laura stays in a hotel, she worries about picking up* (recoger) *bedbugs* (las chinches).

PREPOSITION + INFINITIVE with the reflexive object pronoun

Any verb that immediately follows a preposition must remain in the infinitive. There is no exception to this rule. When the verb is reflexive, the infinitive itself stays untouched, but the reflexive object pronoun changes to agree with the stated or understood subject and is attached to the end of the infinitive. The subject of the reflexive verb usually can be determined from the context of the sentence.

Yo leo **antes de acostarme**.	*I read **before going to bed**.*
Cenamos **después de lavarnos** las manos.	*We eat dinner **after washing** our hands.*
Después de quitarse las botas, él entra en la casa.	***After taking off** his boots, he enters the house.*
Antes de dormirse, ellos cuentan ovejas.	***Before falling asleep**, they count sheep.*
En vez de acostarme, voy a quedarme despierto toda la noche.	***Instead of going to bed**, I'm going to stay awake all night long.*

EJERCICIO 11·3

Complete each sentence with the correct reflexive object pronoun.

1. Antes de vestir_____, yo plancho (*iron*) la ropa.

2. Después de bañar_____, Mariana se acuesta.

3. Antes de ir_____ al trabajo, leemos el periódico.

4. Después de levantar_____, hago la cama.

5. Ellos cenan después de sentar_____.

6. Dorian Gray grita con horror después de ver_____ en el retrato (*portrait*).

7. Después de probar_____ diez vestidos y veinte trajes de baño, Cathy se frustra mucho.

8. Antes de acostar_____, siempre me cepillo los dientes.

9. Antes de afeitar_____, preparas la crema de afeitar.

10. Después de vestir_____, salís para el trabajo.

11. Necesito champú para lavar_____ el pelo.

12. Ella va a bañar_____ en vez de duchar_____ hoy.

Traducción

1. *After getting dressed, I look at myself in the mirror.*

   _____

2. *Before going away, we put on our coats* (el abrigo), *mittens* (la manopla), *and hats.*

   _____

3. *After taking a bath, I put on my robe* (la bata) *and I relax* (relajarse).

   _____

4. *Instead of* (en vez de) *taking a shower, I'm going to take a bath tonight.*

   _____

5. *This soap* (el sabón) *is the best for* (para) *washing your* [sing., formal] *face.*

   _____

6. *I use this shampoo* (el champú) *for washing my hair.*

   _____

7. *When I stay in a hotel, I always request a call* (la llamada) *to* (para) *wake me up.*

   _____

8. *He takes a pill* (la pastilla) *every night in order to* (para) *fall asleep.*

   _____

9. *Some people meditate* (meditar) *in order to relax.*

   _____

10. *You* [pl., informal] *need a razor* (la navaja) *and a blade* (la hoja) *in order to shave (yourselves).*

    _____

Reflexive object pronouns in sentences with two verbs

In a statement or clause that contains two verbs, the first verb is conjugated and the second one remains in the infinitive form. When that second verb is reflexive, the appropriate reflexive object pronoun is attached directly to the infinitive.

Necesito **lavarme** el pelo.	*I need **to wash** my hair.*
Tenemos que **irnos** ahora.	*We have to **leave/go away** now.*
¿Cuándo vas a **acostarte?**	*When are you going to **go to bed**?*
Debéis **quitaros** los zapatos.	*You should **take off** your shoes.*
Ella no puede **verse** en el cristal.	*She can't **see herself** in the glass.*
¿Quieren ustedes **quedarse** aquí?	*Do you want **to stay** here?*

EJERCICIO

¿Verdadero o falso?

_____ 1. Esta noche voy a acostarme a las once y media.

_____ 2. Durante la semana tengo que levantarme antes de las siete de la mañana.

_____ 3. Debo cepillarme los dientes por lo menos tres veces al día.

_____ 4. Me gusta quedarme en hoteles cuando visito otras ciudades.

_____ 5. Prefiero probarme ropa nueva en mi casa y no en el probador (*fitting room*) de una tienda.

_____ 6. Me molesta verme en el espejo (*mirror*) cuando me pruebo trajes de baño en el probador.

_____ 7. Quiero enfermarme mucho este año.

_____ 8. Quiero casarme con una persona famosa y tener fotos de nuestra boda en las revistas *People* y *¡Hola!*

_____ 9. Cuando no puedo dormirme, leo un libro o una revista.

_____ 10. Si no tengo tiempo para ducharme en la mañana, me siento sucio/sucia e incómodo/incómoda todo el día.

_____ 11. No me gusta irme al trabajo sin tomar café primero.

_____ 12. Muchas personas quieren hacerse ricas algún día.

_____ 13. Una persona tiene que quitarse la ropa antes de bañarse.

_____ 14. Muchas personas prefieren quedarse en un hotel económico para ahorrar dinero.

_____ 15. Nadie quiere quedarse en un hotel con ratones, ratas, arañas y todo tipo de insectos.

EJERCICIO

11·5

Traducción

1. *For our honeymoon* (la luna de miel), *we want to stay in an elegant hotel.*

   _____

2. *Where are you* [pl., formal] *going to stay in Paris?*

   _____

3. *I am very warm. I'm going to take off my sweater.*

   _____

4. *I am very cold. I have to put on my coat.*

   _____

5. *No one wants to get sick, but unfortunately* (desgraciadamente) *this happens* (ocurrir).

   _____

6. *Our dog likes to bathe himself in our neighbor's swimming pool. Our neighbor gets angry when our dog does this.*

_____

7. *If you [sing., informal] want to wash your hair, there is shampoo in the cabinet* (el gabinete).

_____

8. *If you [sing., formal] want to shave, the concierge* (el conserje) *can give you a razor* (la navaja) *and some blades* (la hoja).

_____

9. *If you [pl., formal] want to get well* (bien), *you have to eat* (tomar) *this chicken soup* (el caldo de pollo).

_____

10. *You [sing., informal] are going to get sick if you eat that raw* (crudo) *meat.*

_____

EJERCICIO

11·6

Traducción

VOCABULARIO

el bote	(aerosol) can
callarse	to be quiet
fastidioso, fastidiosa	fastidious
la manguera	hose
más a menudo	more often
o… o	either . . . or
quejarse de	to complain about
ya	anymore

"He never bathes anymore! It's absolutely terrible." My neighbor tells me everything, and today she is complaining about her husband. She is a fastidious woman and complains all the time. She tells me that I should wash my hair more often. I tell her that that is my problem and that she should be quiet. She tells me that she can't be quiet when no one in her family bathes or showers. She tells me that after going to bed, she can't fall asleep because she's worrying about all these people who don't wash themselves. I tell her that she can buy herself either a can of Febreze or a hose.

_____

_____

_____

_____

_____

_____

_____

Double-Object Pronoun Order: RID

FUNCTION	To indicate the placement order for two object pronouns in a sentence: reflexive, indirect, direct
SPANISH PLACEMENT	Immediately before the conjugated verb OR attached directly to the infinitive verb, but always in the same order
ENGLISH EQUIVALENTS	Expressions such as "it to me," "them for yourself," "it for myself," "them for you"

The following chart is a review of the reflexive, indirect, and direct object pronouns.

REFLEXIVE		INDIRECT		DIRECT	
me	nos	me	nos	me	nos
te	os	te	os	te	os
se	se	le	les	lo, la	los, las

RID order

When you have two object pronouns in a Spanish sentence, these pronouns always appear in RID order: *reflexive, indirect, direct*. Because the maximum number of pronouns that can appear together is two, the possible combinations are reflexive + indirect (which is rare), reflexive + direct, and indirect + direct. Some examples of the more common combinations are shown below.

Reflexive + Direct

Me lo compro.	*I buy **it for myself**.*
Tu pelo es magnífico.	*Your hair is wonderful.*
¿**Te lo** lavas mucho?	*Do **you** wash **it** a lot?*

Indirect + Direct

Ellos **os los** envían.	*They send **them to you**.*
Yo **te la** escribo.	*I write **it to you**.*
Ella **me las** vende.	*She sells **them to me**.*

EJERCICIO
12·1

Traducción *Unless marked* [f.], it *and* them *are masculine.*
Use the second-person singular Spanish form for English you.

1. *He gives it to me.* _____

2. *She tells it to you.* _____

3. *We give it to you.* _____

4. *I write it* [f.] *to you.* _____

5. *He sends them to us.* _____

6. *We sing it* [f.] *to you.* _____

7. *Why do you give it to me?* _____

8. *Who has it for you?* _____

9. *When do you do it for me?* _____

10. *Why do you tell it to us?* _____

11. *I prepare it* [f.] *for myself.* _____

12. *She buys them* [f.] *for herself.* _____

The "la la" rule

The third-person forms of both the direct and indirect object pronouns, regardless of number or gender, begin with the letter *l*. When they appear together, change the indirect object pronoun **le** (the first pronoun) to **se**. This avoids the singsong, tongue-tripping sound of two small words together starting with the letter *l*. We call this the "la la rule."

Consider the sentence "I give it [*m.*] to him." The indirect object is "him" (**le**) and the direct object is "it" (**lo**). Thus in Spanish we would initially have **Yo le lo doy**. Because of the "la la" rule, however, we change the indirect object pronoun **le** to **se**, and the resulting sentence is **Yo *se* lo doy**.

This change in spelling to accommodate ease of pronunciation could make such a sentence incomprehensible. However, we use pronouns only when their antecedents are understood from the context of the paragraph or conversation. Therefore, while looking at **se lo doy** without any prior knowledge might make the sentence virtually meaningless, knowledge of the referents makes the sentence completely understandable.

Tú conoces a Juan. Será mejor si **se lo** dices tú.	*You know Juan. It will be better if you tell **it to him**.*
Tenemos muchos lápices que no necesitamos. **Se los** damos.	*We have a lot of pencils we don't need. We give **them to you** [sing., formal].*
Los padres de Enrique lo miman. Si él quiere una bicicleta, ellos **se la** compran.	*Enrique's parents spoil him. If he wants a bicycle, they buy **it for him**.*
A mi mamá le fascinan los chocolates. Por eso, **se los** envío.	*My mother loves chocolates. That's why I send **them to her**.*

Traducción *Unless marked [f.], it and them are masculine. Use the second-person singular Spanish form for English* you *unless indicated otherwise.*

1. *He sings it [f.] to her.* _____

2. *We tell it to them.* _____

3. *You buy them for him.* _____

4. *I write it for you [pl., formal].* _____

5. *He sends them to them.* _____

6. *I tell it to her.* _____

7. *He sells it [f.] to her.* _____

8. *You give them [f.] to him.* _____

9. *No one tells it to her.* _____

10. *Why do you tell it to him?* _____

11. *We bring them [f.] to them [f.].* _____

12. *She cooks it for them.* _____

13. *I make them [f.] for you [pl., formal].* _____

14. *Do you make them for them?* _____

15. *Who gives it to them?* _____

Two pronouns in a negative statement

In a negative sentence or clause in which the RID rules apply, place the word "no" (or other word of negation) immediately before the first pronoun. In the examples below, note the effect of the "la la" rule, and watch for sentences like these in the exercises that follow.

No te lo tengo.	*I don't have **it for you**.*
No se los tengo.	*I don't have **them for them**.*
Nunca se la compran.	*They **never** buy **it for her**.*
No nos las vendemos.	*We don't sell **them to ourselves**.*

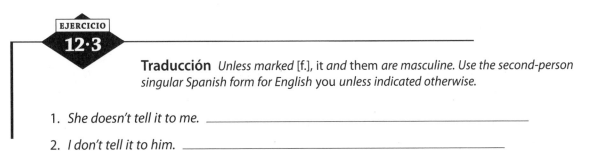

EJERCICIO
12·3

Traducción *Unless marked [f.], it and them are masculine. Use the second-person singular Spanish form for English* you *unless indicated otherwise.*

1. *She doesn't tell it to me.* _____

2. *I don't tell it to him.* _____

3. *We don't buy them [f.] for ourselves.* _____

4. *They don't send it [f.] to us on time* (a tiempo).

_____

5. *She doesn't make it for us every day.* _____

6. *I don't give it [f.] to them.* _____

7. *He doesn't pay me for it in cash* (en efectivo).

_____

8. *He doesn't give it to me on time.* _____

9. *Why don't you send it [f.] to her tomorrow?*

_____

10. *Don't you buy them [f.] for them every day?*

_____

11. *I never buy them for myself.* _____

12. *We never tell them to her.* _____

Two pronouns in sentences with two verbs

In a statement or clause that contains two verbs, the first verb is conjugated and the second one remains in the infinitive form. The placement of the two object pronouns follows the same pattern that has been seen with individual pronouns. The object pronouns—kept together—may either be placed before the conjugated verb or attached directly to the infinitive. In addition, they always appear in RID order: reflexive, indirect, direct.

In these examples, the two pronouns are placed before the conjugated verb.

me las quiere entregar	*he wants to give **them to me***
nos los debe vender	*he ought to sell **them to us***
se lo podemos mostrar	*we can show **it to them***

Note that the "la la" rule comes into play in third-person situations.

When the two object pronouns are attached directly to the infinitive, a written accent must be added in order for the infinitive to retain its natural stress, which always falls on the final syllable. Therefore, a written accent is placed over the vowel in the stressed syllable of the infinitive.

entregar + me + las > **entregármelas**	*to give them to me*
vender + nos + los > **vendérnoslos**	*to sell them to us*
mostrar + se + lo > **mostrárselo**	*to show it to them*

Te lo quiero **dar.** Quiero **dártelo.**	*I want **to give it to you**.*
Se lo queremos **decir.** Queremos **decírselo.**	*We want **to say it to him**.*
Me la tienes que **enviar.** Tienes que **enviármela.**	*You have **to send it to me**.*
Os lo necesitáis **poner.** Necesitáis **ponéroslo.**	*You need **to put it on yourselves**.*

Ella **se lo** puede **hacer**. }
Ella puede **hacérselo**.

*She can **do it for herself**.*

Ustedes **nos lo** pueden **esconder**. }
Ustedes pueden **escondérnoslo**.

*You can **hide it from us**.*

Traducción *Express each of the following statements in two complete sentences showing the two options for placement of the object pronouns. Unless marked [f.], it and them are masculine. Use the second-person singular Spanish form for English you unless indicated otherwise.*

1. *I want to tell it to you.*

   _____

   _____

2. *I want to buy it [f.] for you.*

   _____

   _____

3. *You have to give it to me.*

   _____

   _____

4. *We have to sell them to you.*

   _____

   _____

5. *We have to sell it to her.*

   _____

   _____

6. *They should buy them [f.] for you.*

   _____

   _____

7. *They should buy it for themselves.*

   _____

   _____

8. *She needs to send it [f.] to me.*

   _____

   _____

Double-Object Pronoun Order: RID **99**

9. *You [pl., formal]* have to give it [f.] *to us.*

_____

_____

10. *I should bring it to them.*

_____

_____

11. *They should give them [f.] to me.*

_____

_____

12. *She wants to sing it [f.] for us.*

_____

_____

13. *You can send it to me by mail* (por correo).

_____

_____

14. *He can pay you for it [f.] in cash.*

_____

_____

15. *I want to pay you [pl., informal]* for them by check (con un cheque).

_____

_____

Questions and negative statements with two verbs

In a negative sentence with two verbs, place the word "no" (or other word of negation) before the conjugated verb. If you also place the pronouns before the conjugated verb, the word "no" precedes the pronouns. If you attach the pronouns to the infinitive, the word "no" immediately precedes the conjugated verb.

For questions, add question marks but maintain the order of the sentence elements (subject and verb).

To add the subject (either a noun or pronoun) to a negative statement or a question, place it at the very beginning of the sentence. It should always be placed before the conjugated verb; it should appear before the "no" if the statement or question is negative.

No **te lo** quiero **dejar**. No quiero **dejártelo**. }	*I don't want **to leave it for you**.*
No **se lo** tenemos que **comprar**. No tenemos que **comprárselo**. }	*We don't have **to buy it for him**.*

¿**Me lo** quieres **dejar**? ¿Quieres **dejármelo**?	}	*Do you want **to leave it for me**?*
¿**Me lo** podéis **escribir**? ¿Podéis **escribírmelo**?	}	*Can you **write it for me**?*
¿Marcos no **se lo** necesita **regalar**? ¿Marcos no necesita **regalárselo**?	}	*Doesn't Marcos need **to give it to her**?*
Ellos nunca **se lo** saben **decir**. Ellos nunca saben **decírselo**.	}	*They never know how **to tell it to her**.*

EJERCICIO
12·5

Traducción *Express each of the following statements in two complete sentences showing the two options for placement of the object pronouns. Unless marked [f.], it and them are masculine. Use the second-person singular Spanish form for English you unless indicated otherwise.*

1. *Can you do it for me?*

_____

_____

2. *No, I can't do it for you.*

_____

_____

3. *Do we have to tell it [f.] to him?*

_____

_____

4. *When do you want to give them [f.] to them?*

_____

_____

5. *You don't need to pay me for it now.*

_____

_____

6. *They can't sell it to you in the United States.*

_____

_____

7. *We can't sell it [f.] to them at this price.*

_____

_____

8. *When do you want to tell it to me?*

_____

_____

9. *Aren't you going to bring it to us today?*

_____

_____

10. *Can't they send them [f.] to us by mail (por correo)?*

_____

_____

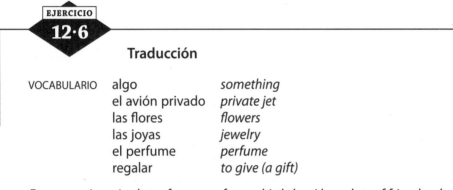

EJERCICIO
12·6

Traducción

VOCABULARIO		
	algo	*something*
	el avión privado	*private jet*
	las flores	*flowers*
	las joyas	*jewelry*
	el perfume	*perfume*
	regalar	*to give (a gift)*

Every year I receive lots of presents for my birthday. I have lots of friends who have stores, and they always give me what they sell or what they make. And for their birthdays, I always give them presents too. My friend Merlin sells flowers, and he gives them to me. Manolo sells shoes, and he gives them to me. Juan sells coffee, and he gives it to me. Oribe sells shampoo, and he gives it to me. Coco makes perfume, and she sends it to me, because she lives in France. Stella makes dresses, and she sends them to me. Harry makes jewelry, and he always makes me something special for my birthday. This year I want a private jet. Who is going to give it to me?

_____

_____

_____

_____

_____

_____

_____

_____

_____

Reciprocal Pronouns

FUNCTION	To indicate an action that goes back and forth between two or more subjects
SPANISH PLACEMENT	Immediately before the conjugated verb OR attached directly to the infinitive
ENGLISH EQUIVALENTS	"each other," "one another," "ourselves," "yourselves," "themselves"

The term *reciprocity* indicates that an action is reciprocal, or occurring between or among all the interested parties in an equal manner. If I see you, but you don't see me, there is no reciprocity. However, when we see each other, the action is *reciprocal.*

Since reciprocity occurs only when two or more persons are involved, the reciprocal pronouns exist only in the plural forms. Thus, the phrases "each other" and "one another" are frequently used in sentences involving reciprocal pronouns. The pronouns used to express reciprocity are identical to the plural reflexive pronouns.

nos	*ourselves, each other, one another*
os	*yourselves, each other, one another*
se	*themselves, yourselves, each other, one another*

NOTE All rules of syntax that apply to reflexive pronouns also apply to reciprocal pronouns.

People often stumble over when to use "each other" and "one another" in English. Because of the reciprocal pronoun **se**, this is not an issue in Spanish. In English, the distinction is simple: Use "each other" when referring to precisely two people; use "one another" when referring to more than two people. Learn and employ this distinction now so that you come across as the intelligent person you are.

Nos vemos cada día.	*We see each other every day.*
¿**Os conocéis** bien?	*Do you know one another well?*
Ellos **no pueden escribirse** muy a menudo.	*They can't write to one another very often.*
Siempre **nos encontramos** en el supermercado pero **nunca nos hablamos**.	*We always run into each other at the supermarket, but we never speak (to each other).*

Complete each sentence with the correct reciprocal pronoun. (Hint: The conjugated verb provides a clue.) Then translate the sentence into English.

1. _____ conocemos muy bien.

   _____

2. Ellos _____ quieren mucho.

   _____

3. _____ veis por la ventana.

   _____

4. ¿_____ conocen ustedes?

   _____

5. _____ besan cada mañana.

   _____

6. Cada día _____ decimos "te quiero."

   _____

7. Cuando ellos están enojados, no _____ hablan.

   _____

8. ¿_____ visitáis con frecuencia?

   _____

9. Ellos _____ pelean (*fight*) mucho porque _____ odian.

   _____

10. _____ hablamos por teléfono tres veces cada semana.

    _____

11. Ellos quieren conocer_____ mejor.

    _____

12. No podemos ver_____ tan a menudo como queremos.

    _____

Traducción

1. *We write long letters to each other every week.*

   _____

2. *When do you* [pl., informal] *see each other?*

   _____

3. *Why do they yell at* (gritar) *each other so much?*

   _____

4. *The lovebirds* (los tórtolos) *sing to each other in the treetop* (la copa del árbol).

   _____

5. *We buy one another gifts every December.*

   _____

6. *The five friends run into one another* (encontrarse) *at the gym* (el gimnasio) *every Friday afternoon.*

   _____

7. *We can't speak to each other because my cell phone doesn't work* (funcionar).

   _____

8. *You* [pl., formal] *shouldn't tell each other everything. He can't keep* (guardar) *a secret.*

   _____

9. *You* [pl., informal] *can look at each other now.*

   _____

10. *My neighbors yell at one another every Saturday night.*

    _____

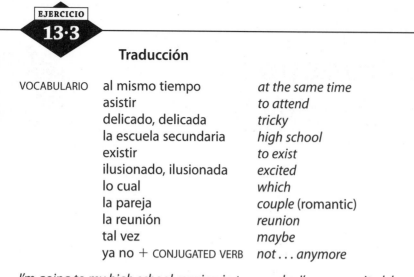

EJERCICIO

13·3

Traducción

VOCABULARIO
al mismo tiempo	*at the same time*
asistir	*to attend*
delicado, delicada	*tricky*
la escuela secundaria	*high school*
existir	*to exist*
ilusionado, ilusionada	*excited*
lo cual	*which*
la pareja	*couple* (romantic)
la reunión	*reunion*
tal vez	*maybe*
ya no + CONJUGATED VERB	*not . . . anymore*

I'm going to my high school reunion in two weeks. I'm very excited, because Henry is going to attend. I know this because Laura, my best friend, is the secretary of the class. She and I talk to each other every week, and she tells me everything. These reunions are tricky. We want to see one another, but at the same time we don't want to see one another. Or, maybe, we want to see one another in the past, which doesn't exist anymore. It's especially hard for romantic couples. Some former couples see each other after many years, and it is wonderful. But there are other ex-couples who see each other, and it's a horrible experience.

_____

_____

_____

_____

_____

_____

_____

_____

_____

The Pronoun **Se** and the Passive Voice

FUNCTION	To indicate that an action is performed by an unspecified subject
SPANISH PLACEMENT	Immediately before the conjugated verb in the third-person singular and plural only
ENGLISH EQUIVALENTS	"it," "you," "we," "they," "one," "anybody," "a person," etc.

The passive voice

The passive voice is used to describe an action that is carried out but has no specific, identified agent. For example, in the sentence "The doors are unlocked at 5:30," there is no identified subject or agent. We don't know *who* actually unlocks the doors. The following examples contrast the active and passive voices.

ACTIVE VOICE	PASSIVE VOICE
Paul **closes** the shop at 9:00.	The shop **is closed** at 9:00.
Sue **heard** a baby crying.	A baby's cries **were heard**.
The wind **blew** down the tree.	The tree **was blown** down.

Each sentence in the active voice has a specific subject, but the corresponding sentence in the passive voice has an unspecified subject: we don't know *who* closes the shop, *who* heard the baby's cries, or *what* blew down the tree.

There are two ways to express the passive voice in Spanish: (1) using a form of **ser** and a participle and (2) using **se** and a conjugated form of the verb.

Joaquín **es respetado.**	
Se respeta a Joaquín.	*Joaquín **is respected**.*
La fortaleza **fue destruida.**	
La fortaleza **se destruyó.**	*The fortress **was destroyed**.*

In both of these examples, the passive voice expresses the result of an action, but not the agent or performer of the action. At times the actor/agent is not known; other times, naming the person is irrelevant.

Formation of the passive voice with **se**

To use **se** as a substitute for the passive voice in Spanish, place **se** before the conjugated verb in the third person. If the noun following the verb is singular, conjugate the verb in the third-person singular. If that noun is plural or if there is a series of nouns, conjugate the verb in the third-person plural.

Se habla español en México.
Se hablan inglés y francés en Canadá.
Se vende plata en esta joyería.
No se venden joyas aquí.
Las historietas no se consideran obras
     literarias.

Spanish *is spoken* in Mexico.
English and French *are spoken* in Canada.
Silver *is sold* at this jewelry store.
Jewels **are** not **sold** here.
Comic books **are** not **considered** literary works.

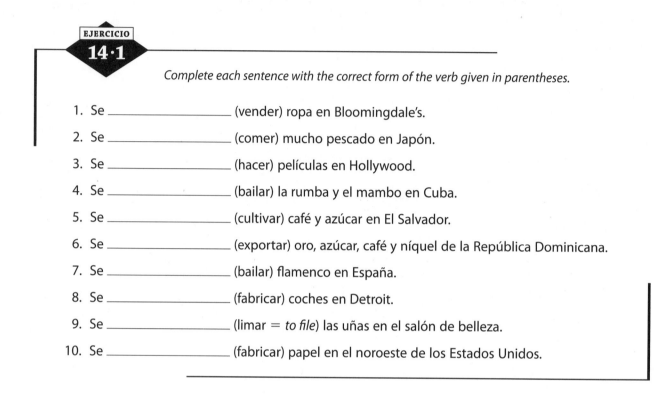

EJERCICIO
14·1

Complete each sentence with the correct form of the verb given in parentheses.

1. Se _____ (vender) ropa en Bloomingdale's.

2. Se _____ (comer) mucho pescado en Japón.

3. Se _____ (hacer) películas en Hollywood.

4. Se _____ (bailar) la rumba y el mambo en Cuba.

5. Se _____ (cultivar) café y azúcar en El Salvador.

6. Se _____ (exportar) oro, azúcar, café y níquel de la República Dominicana.

7. Se _____ (bailar) flamenco en España.

8. Se _____ (fabricar) coches en Detroit.

9. Se _____ (limar = *to file*) las uñas en el salón de belleza.

10. Se _____ (fabricar) papel en el noroeste de los Estados Unidos.

EJERCICIO
14·2

Traducción

1. *Spanish is spoken here.*

   _____

2. *Spanish and French are spoken here.*

   _____

3. *Shoes are sold there.*

   _____

4. *Fireworks* (los fuegos artificiales) *and liquor* (los licores) *are not sold to teenagers* (el adolescente).

   _____

5. *Entrance* (la entrada) *is not permitted* (permitir) *before 10:00.*

   _____

6. *Cameras are not permitted in the theater.*

   _____

7. *Gold and jewels are not considered good investments* (la inversión).

   _____

8. *The restaurants and the museums are closed on Mondays.*

   _____

9. *The bank is closed at two thirty.*

   _____

10. *Piñatas are made* (fabricar) *in this factory* (la fábrica).

   _____

Using **se** to indicate an impersonal subject

In Spanish, as in English, an impersonal subject is frequently used. In Spanish, **se** is used to indicate an impersonal subject—both singular and plural. For example, in the sentence **Se baila la cumbia en Colombia** ("They dance the cumbia in Colombia"), we don't know specifically who "they" are. There are no names or faces attached. The subject could refer to many people in general, but in fact refers to no one in particular.

In English, another common impersonal subject is the word "you," as in "You shouldn't call people after nine." Other frequently used impersonal subjects in English include "one," "it," "people," "anybody," and "no one," some of which are singular and some plural. All of these ways of expressing impersonal subjects in English are covered in Spanish by the pronoun **se**.

No se debe matar.	*One shouldn't kill.* / *You shouldn't kill.*
¡Así **se hace**!	*That's how **it's done**!* / *That's how **you do it**!*
¿Qué **se puede hacer**?	*What's **a person to do**?* / *What **can one do**?*
Jamás se explicó el asesinato.	***They never explained** the murder.* / ***No one ever explained** the murder.*
En este club **se baila** la cumbia y el mambo, pero no la Macarena.	*In this club, **they dance** the cumbia and the mambo, but not the Macarena.* / *In this club, **people dance** the cumbia and the mambo, but not the Macarena.*

Note that in the examples above showing an impersonal subject, the third-person singular form of the verb is always used in Spanish, even in those cases when the English expression uses a plural verb. However, in Spanish, when the third-person plural form of the verb is used to express the same concept, the reflexive **se** can be dropped, as shown in the examples below.

Se me conoce aquí. / **Me conocen** aquí.	*They know me here.*
Aquí **se produce** el mejor café. / Aquí **producen** el mejor café.	*They produce the best coffee here.*
Se dice que **no se puede** fumar en ninguna parte. / **Dicen** que **no se puede** fumar en ninguna parte.	*They say that you can't smoke anywhere.*

Most platitudes employ an impersonal subject with the **se** construction, as shown in the example below.

Se puede dirigir un caballo al agua... *You can lead* a horse to water . . .

Traducción

1. *You should pay your taxes* (los impuestos) *every April.*

_____

2. *You can't be in two places at the same time* (al mismo tiempo).

_____

3. *You need to change the oil* (el aceite) *in your car every* (cada) *three thousand miles.*

_____

4. *One shouldn't blame* (culpar) *others for the results* (el resultado) *of his/her actions.*

_____

5. *One should exercise* (hacer ejercicio) *and meditate* (meditar) *daily.*

_____

6. *They should make these maps clearer. You can't read this!*

_____

7. *You can't get* (extraer) *blood from a turnip* (el nabo).

_____

8. *You can't judge* (juzgar) *a book by its cover* (la portada).

_____

9. *People should brush their teeth after* (después de) *eating and before going to bed.*

_____

10. *You can swim and play tennis in this club.*

_____

11. *In order to dance La Bamba, you need a little bit of grace* (una poca de gracia).

_____

12. *They never explained the UFOs* (el OVNI).

_____

13. *Can one go in* (entrar)? *What time do they open the doors?*

_____

14. *In this store, people pay a fixed price* (un precio fijo).

_____

15. *It is said that you should look before* (antes de) *you leap* (saltar).

_____

The passive voice with inanimate objects

We often speak of actions that take place for which there is no—or at least no apparent—human element involved in the action, for example, "My car breaks down on me every winter." We also refer to actions that clearly are performed by humans, but for which the mention of those humans is irrelevant—for example, "The store opens at 10:00."

In such situations, we use the passive voice, which allows us to ignore the performer of the action and focus on the action itself. If the noun is singular, use the singular form of the verb; if the noun is plural, use the plural form.

Se abre la tienda a las diez.
La tienda se abre a las diez. } *The store opens* at ten.

Se abren las tiendas a las diez.
Las tiendas se abren a las diez. } *The stores open* at ten.

Se estropea mi coche cada invierno.
Mi coche se estropea cada invierno. } *My car breaks down* every winter.

Se arreglan los pantalones en esta sastrería.
Los pantalones se arreglan en esta sastrería. } *Pants are fixed* in this tailor's shop.

Note that the noun can either precede or follow the verb.

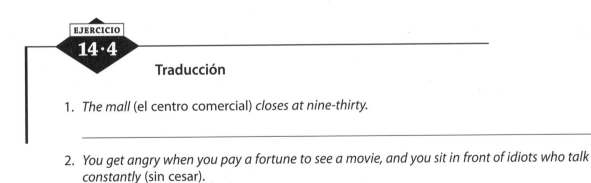

EJERCICIO
14·4

Traducción

1. *The mall* (el centro comercial) *closes at nine-thirty.*

_____

2. *You get angry when you pay a fortune to see a movie, and you sit in front of idiots who talk constantly* (sin cesar).

_____

3. *Lightbulbs* (la bombilla) *usually burn out* (quemarse) *after one hundred hours.*

_____

4. *When a car breaks down* (estropearse) *on the freeway* (la autopista), *it's a catastrophe* (el catástrofe) *for everyone.*

_____

5. *What time does that restaurant open?*

_____

6. *The sun sets* (ponerse) *at 8:30 P.M. in the summer.*

_____

7. *With this appliance* (el aparato), *your lights turn on* (encenderse) *and turn off* (apagarse) *automatically* (automáticamente).

_____

8. *After the holidays* (los días de fiesta), *millions of toys break* (romperse).

_____

9. *When she sings, all the glasses break* (quebrarse).

_____

10. *The museums close at six sharp* (en punto).

_____

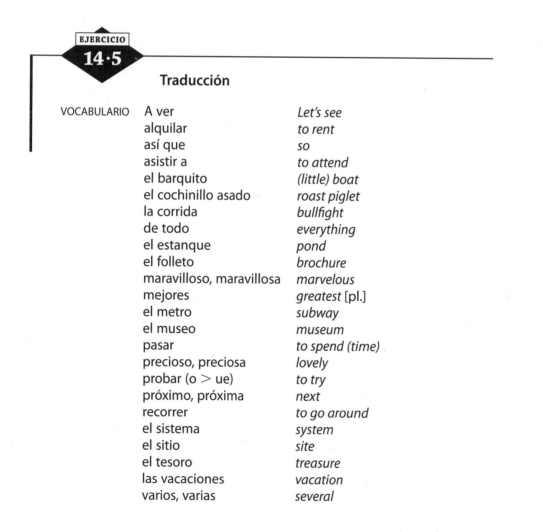

EJERCICIO

14·5

Traducción

VOCABULARIO	A ver	*Let's see*
	alquilar	*to rent*
	así que	*so*
	asistir a	*to attend*
	el barquito	*(little) boat*
	el cochinillo asado	*roast piglet*
	la corrida	*bullfight*
	de todo	*everything*
	el estanque	*pond*
	el folleto	*brochure*
	maravilloso, maravillosa	*marvelous*
	mejores	*greatest* [pl.]
	el metro	*subway*
	el museo	*museum*
	pasar	*to spend (time)*
	precioso, preciosa	*lovely*
	probar (o > ue)	*to try*
	próximo, próxima	*next*
	recorrer	*to go around*
	el sistema	*system*
	el sitio	*site*
	el tesoro	*treasure*
	las vacaciones	*vacation*
	varios, varias	*several*

112 PRONOUNS

I want to go to Madrid for my next vacation. I have a brochure with me now. Let's see! What can a person do in Madrid? They say here that the Prado is one of the world's greatest museums and that you can spend several days exploring its treasures. It says that in Madrid the subway system is very good, so one doesn't need to rent a car. You can take the subway to all the sites in the city. If you go to a good restaurant in Madrid, you can try roast piglet. Also, El Retiro is a lovely park, and people can rent little boats to go around the pond. You can attend the bullfights because Spain is one of the few countries where it is still legal, and you can dance until five o'clock in the morning. You can do everything in this marvelous city!

_____

_____

_____

_____

_____

_____

_____

_____

PREPOSITIONS

Prepositions and Prepositional Phrases

15

A *preposition* is the part of speech that shows the relationship of a noun or pronoun to another word in a phrase, clause, or sentence.

Prepositions are often referred to as "those little words." But they are little words that mean a lot, because prepositions reveal place, time, direction, manner, and connection, among other things. Compound prepositions are made up of multiple "little words" that express one prepositional meaning.

Because prepositions are specific in meaning, it is important to study them in depth. As a rule, you cannot substitute one preposition for another, so it is important to know precisely which preposition to use in a given situation.

For the most part, prepositions are used to show the relationships between nouns and pronouns.

Estoy **con** Carlota.	*I am **with** Carlota.*
Roberto está **cerca de** mi casa.	*Roberto is **near** my house.*
¿Estás **en** el hospital?	*You are **in** the hospital?*
El gato está **encima del** estante.	*The cat is **on top of** the bookshelf.*

Each of the prepositions used in the examples above shows the relationship between the subject of the sentence ("I," "Roberto," "you," "cat") and the object of the preposition ("Carlota," "house," "hospital," "bookshelf"). The preposition and its object together form a prepositional phrase.

To change a preposition is to change the meaning of the sentence entirely, as is shown in the sentences that follow.

Estoy **lejos de** Carlota.	*I am **far from** Carlota.*
Roberto está **en** mi casa.	*Roberto is **in** my house.*
¿Estás **al lado del** hospital?	*You are **next door to** the hospital?*
El gato está **detrás del** estante.	*The cat is **behind** the bookshelf.*

The nouns and pronouns in the examples above are linked by the preposition itself, but they are also linked by a verb, often the verb "to be." (In Spanish, depending on the context, the linking verb is either **ser** or **estar**.) In these examples, you find "I *am*," "Roberto *is*," "you *are*," "the cat *is*."

Functions of prepositional phrases

Prepositional phrases can perform many different functions in a sentence. At times, a prepositional phrase modifies a noun and has an adjectival function, often identifying "*Which one?*" Other times, a prepositional phrase modifies a verb and has an adverbial function, such as answering the question "*Where?*" Although the prepositional phrase itself may not change, its use in the sentence does. Note the differences in the examples that follow.

Prepositional phrase used as an adjective ("Which one?")

El coche **en el garaje** es azul.   *The car **in the garage** is blue.*
John es el muchacho **detrás de la pared**.   *John is the boy **behind the wall**.*

Prepositional phrase used as an adverb ("Where?")

El coche está **en el garaje**.   *The car is **in the garage**.*
John camina **detrás de la pared**.   *John walks **behind the wall**.*

Prepositions that show a relationship between nouns and/or pronouns

The principal function of a preposition is to demonstrate the relationship between two or more people or things. This relationship can be abstract, as in "He sings songs *about* love," or it can be physical and concrete, as in "The book is *on* the table."

Escribe poemas **acerca del** amor.   *She writes poems **about** love.*
Quiero un libro **sobre** la economía.   *I want a book **on** economics.*
La silla está **contra** la pared.   *The chair is **against** the wall.*
Además de los tacos, Lola prepara la salsa.   ***In addition to** the tacos, Lola prepares the salsa.*

Below are several frequently used prepositions, which are used in the exercises that follow.

VOCABULARIO	
acerca de	about
además de	besides, in addition to
con	with
contra	against
en lugar de	instead of
en vez de	instead of
excepto	except
menos	except
salvo	except
según	according to
sin	without
sobre	about, on (*topic*)

¿Cuál es verdadero o falso para ti?

_____ 1. Yo sé mucho acerca de Hollywood.

_____ 2. Me gusta el té con limón y azúcar.

_____ 3. En la Serie Mundial, la Liga Nacional juega contra la Liga Americana.

_____ 4. Según mi mejor amigo/amiga, un día sin café es un día sin valor.

_____ 5. Yo como todo tipo de comida, excepto chocolate.

_____ 6. Aristóteles escribió ensayos sobre filosofía.

_____ 7. Yo estudio matemáticas además de español.

_____ 8. Según la Biblia, Adán y Eva fueron las primeras personas del mundo.

_____ 9. Siempre dejo mis zapatos contra la pared.

_____ 10. Tengo un libro sobre la historia de Francia.

_____ 11. Me gusta oír noticias acerca de mis amigos.

_____ 12. Además de ropa, Bloomingdale's vende muebles, coches y refrigeradores.

_____ 13. Yo soy una persona sin problemas.

_____ 14. Nadie, menos los niños pequeños, cree que existe Santa Claus.

_____ 15. En este momento estoy con mi mejor amigo/amiga.

_____ 16. Tomo té en vez de café.

Traducción *Use the second-person singular Spanish form for English* you.

1. *He always talks about his girlfriend.*

   _____

2. *I prefer coffee with milk and sugar.*

   _____

3. *He prefers tea without sugar.*

   _____

4. Don Quijote *is the best novel in the world, according to José.*

   _____

5. *In addition to flowers, her boyfriend gives her candy* (los dulces) *on every date* (la cita).

   _____

6. *The director's back* (la espalda) *is against the wall.*

_____

7. *This book is about George Washington.*

_____

8. *They don't write much about their problems.*

_____

9. *Do you want pizza with meat* (la carne) *or without meat?*

_____

10. *I like everything here except the shoes.*

_____

11. *His thesis* (la tesis) *is about the art of Rome.*

_____

12. *According to Julia, her friends know nothing about classical music.*

_____

13. *I want everything against the wall, except the podium* (el podio).

_____

14. *You have to serve the drinks* (la bebida) *in addition to the food.*

_____

15. *The library doesn't have anything about the history of pizza.*

_____

Prepositions of location

A very common function of the preposition is to tell where someone or something is located physically in relation to someone or something else—for example, "The bike is *in front of* the house" and "Mario is *to the left of* Susana."

Several of the prepositions of location are made up of more than one word. These are called compound prepositions. They must be followed by a noun or a pronoun just as one-word prepositions are.

El coche está **delante de** la casa.	*The car is **in front of** the house.*
Juan está **a la derecha de** Carmen.	*Juan is **to the right of** Carmen.*

Note that because these prepositions show location, the verb **estar** is frequently used.

There is one exception to using **estar** to show location: when telling where an event takes place, use **ser**.

LOCATION	María **está en** el teatro.	*María is in the theater.*
EVENT	El concierto **es en** el teatro.	*The concert is in the theater.* OR
		The concert is at the theater.

Understanding the Spanish en

It is important to understand the Spanish preposition **en**, which expresses the English meanings "in," "on," "into," and "at." Prepositions in Spanish can have very literal meanings. For example, to express in English that you have a job with the Harrods department store, you would probably say, "I work *at* Harrods." The reality, however, is that when you are working, you are physically *in* the Harrods store, and so to express the same idea in Spanish, you would say, **Trabajo *en* Harrods**. See the sentences below for more examples of how Spanish **en** can be expressed in English.

Estoy **en** su casa.	*I am **in** his house.*
El cuadro está **en** la pared.	*The painting is **on** the wall.*
Ella echa jugo **en** los vasos.	*She pours juice **into** the glasses.*
Estoy **en** la puerta de su casa.	*I am **at** the door of his house.*
Miro los retratos **en** el museo.	*I look at the portraits **at** the museum.*
Compro mi ropa **en** Bloomingdale's.	*I buy my clothing **at** Bloomingdale's.*

Below are several frequently used prepositions of location.

VOCABULARIO

a	at
a la derecha de	to the right of
a la izquierda de	to the left of
a través de	across
al lado de	next to, next door to
cerca de	near, close to, by
con	with
debajo de	under
delante de	in front of
dentro de	inside
detrás de	behind
en	in, on, into, at
encima de	on top of
enfrente de	across from, opposite
entre (*dos personas o cosas*)	between (*two people or things*)
entre (*varias personas o cosas*)	among (*several people or things*)
frente a	facing
fuera de	outside
junto a	by, next to, next door to
lejos de	far from
sobre	on top of, above

EJERCICIO

¿Cuál es verdadero o falso para ti?

_____ 1. Hay un árbol delante de mi casa.

_____ 2. En mi sala, hay una lámpara a la izquierda del sofá.

_____ 3. Mi coche está dentro del garaje ahora.

_____ 4. Hay una araña de luces (*chandelier*) sobre la mesa en el comedor.

_____ 5. Hay mucho polvo (*dust*) debajo de mi cama.

_____ 6. Alguien está a la derecha de mí ahora.

_____ 7. Hay un farol (*streetlight*) fuera de mi ventana.

_____ 8. Vivo cerca de una biblioteca pública.

_____ 9. El garaje está detrás de mi casa.

_____ 10. Mi mejor amigo/amiga vive enfrente de un restaurante.

_____ 11. Canadá está lejos de Europa.

_____ 12. El estado de Kansas está entre los estados Colorado y Missouri.

_____ 13. Usualmente, se juega un partido de béisbol en un estadio.

_____ 14. Al lado de mi casa hay un jardín.

_____ 15. Los pájaros encima de mi casa mejoran la belleza del barrio.

_____ 16. En la corte, los abogados están frente al juez (*judge*).

EJERCICIO
15·2

Traducción *Use the second-person singular Spanish form for English* you.

1. *There is a book on top of the table.*

   _____

2. *John is to the right of me, and Felipe is to the left of Elena.*

   _____

3. *Do you live next door to our restaurant?*

   _____

4. *Every spring we plant* (sembrar) *flowers in front of the house.*

   _____

5. *We need more light* (la iluminación) *above the paintings* (el cuadro).

   _____

6. *People* (la gente) *across the country watch* (mirar) *the Olympics* (los juegos olímpicos) *on television.*

   _____

7. *My favorite song is "Close to You."*

   _____

8. *Many people want to live far from the airport* (el aeropuerto).

   _____

9. *Do you know that there is a tiger* (el tigre) *under your bed?*

_____

10. *Why are there so many* (tanto) *dogs outside your house?*

_____

11. *Who is in the kitchen with Dinah?*

_____

12. *What do you have inside your mouth?*

_____

13. *He works at the bank.*

_____

14. *They are in the bank.*

_____

15. *There isn't anything on television tonight.*

_____

16. *There is nothing between us.*

_____

17. *Who is behind you?*

_____

18. *One watches movies in the theater.*

_____

Prepositions of movement

In addition to telling "*Which one?*" and "*Where?*", prepositions can indicate movement—where someone or something is going. In the sentences that follow, the same prepositional phrase (**a lo largo de**, meaning "along") has an adjectival function in the first sentence and an adverbial function in the second, where it indicates movement in addition to location.

Plantamos flores **alrededor del** monumento.

We plant flowers **around** the monument.

Ayer, caminé **a lo largo de** la playa.

*Yesterday, I walked **along** the beach.*

Below are several frequently used prepositions that indicate movement.

VOCABULARIO	
a lo largo de	along
alrededor de	around
hacia	toward
más allá de	beyond
por	through, throughout

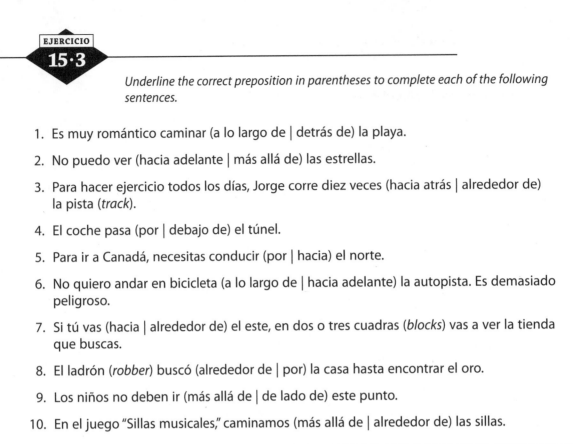

EJERCICIO 15·3

Underline the correct preposition in parentheses to complete each of the following sentences.

1. Es muy romántico caminar (a lo largo de | detrás de) la playa.

2. No puedo ver (hacia adelante | más allá de) las estrellas.

3. Para hacer ejercicio todos los días, Jorge corre diez veces (hacia atrás | alrededor de) la pista (*track*).

4. El coche pasa (por | debajo de) el túnel.

5. Para ir a Canadá, necesitas conducir (por | hacia) el norte.

6. No quiero andar en bicicleta (a lo largo de | hacia adelante) la autopista. Es demasiado peligroso.

7. Si tú vas (hacia | alrededor de) el este, en dos o tres cuadras (*blocks*) vas a ver la tienda que buscas.

8. El ladrón (*robber*) buscó (alrededor de | por) la casa hasta encontrar el oro.

9. Los niños no deben ir (más allá de | de lado de) este punto.

10. En el juego "Sillas musicales," caminamos (más allá de | alrededor de) las sillas.

EJERCICIO 15·4

Traducción *Use the second-person singular Spanish form for English* you.

1. *I run around the lake every morning.*

   _____

2. *Do you walk along the boulevard (el bulevar)?*

   _____

3. *The detective searches throughout the house.*

   _____

4. *He's always looking toward his goals (la meta).*

   _____

5. *Superman can fly (volar) through the air.*

   _____

6. *Every evening they walk through the mall (el centro comercial).*

   _____

7. *If you look beyond that tree, you can see the roller coaster* (la montaña rusa).

_____

8. *Do you want to walk around the block* (la cuadra) *with me?*

_____

9. *You can't go beyond the end* (el final) *of this block.*

_____

10. *We can drive* (conducir) *toward the river and then walk along the path* (la senda).

_____

11. *Nathan Chen can skate* (patinar) *forward and backward.*

_____

12. *Superman can fly, but he doesn't fly backwards.*

_____

Prepositions of geographical orientation

To give geographical directions or to describe location in geographical terms requires a prepositional phrase in Spanish. Note that in English, we often say "north of" instead of "to the north of." When using the Spanish expressions, however, be sure to keep the complete phrase in mind. Below are several frequently used prepositions that indicate geographical orientation.

VOCABULARIO	
al este de	(to the) east of
al nordeste/noreste de	(to the) northeast of
al noroeste de	(to the) northwest of
al norte de	(to the) north of
al oeste de	(to the) west of
al sudeste/sureste de	(to the) southeast of
al sudoeste/suroeste de	(to the) southwest of
al sur de	(to the) south of

Hay una gasolinera **al norte del** supermercado.

*There's a gas station **north of** the supermarket.*

La mina está **al nordeste del** bosque.

*The mine is **to the northeast of** the forest.*

Look at the map of the central United States below. With Missouri as your point of reference, answer the following questions with a complete sentence, using prepositions of geographical location. (The first item has been done for you.)

1. ¿Dónde está Iowa?   *Iowa está al norte de Missouri.*

2. ¿Dónde está Arkansas? _____

3. ¿Dónde está Kansas? _____

4. ¿Dónde está Illinois? _____

5. ¿Dónde está Michigan? _____

6. ¿Dónde está Nebraska? _____

7. ¿Dónde está Oklahoma? _____

8. ¿Dónde está Tennessee? _____

9. ¿Dónde está Louisiana? _____

10. ¿Dónde está Minnesota? _____

Prepositions of origin and destination

Prepositions are used to express origin and destination. In actuality, these prepositions are variations of prepositions that show movement. Think of these prepositions as revealing motion in time. Mentally, to reach the origin of something, you move toward the past; to reach a destination, you move toward the future. Below are several frequently used prepositions that indicate origin and destination.

Origin

a causa de	because of, for
de	from, of
de (*to indicate authorship*)	by
desde	(all the way) from
por	because of, for
por (*to indicate authorship*)	by

Destination

a	to
hacia	toward
para (*purpose or destination*)	for

| ORIGIN | Me encantan los poemas **de** Gabriela Mistral. | *I love the poems **by** Gabriela Mistral.* |
| DESTINATION | Salen **para** Francia mañana. | *They leave **for** France tomorrow.* |

EJERCICIO

15·6

Traducción *Unless otherwise indicated, use the second-person singular Spanish form for English* you.

1. *Because of COVID* (la pandemia del COVID-19), *I can't go to the movies with my friends.*

_____

2. *I'm reading a book by John Steinbeck.*

_____

3. *This book is for you* [pl., formal].

_____

4. *Greetings (all the way) from Cancún!*

_____

5. *We're going to the mall* (el centro comercial). *Do you want to go with us?*

_____

6. *These pearls* (la perla) *are from Japan.*

_____

7. *All my friends from college* (la universidad) *are here.*

_____

8. *What do they want from me?*

_____

9. *I don't have anything for you.*

_____

10. *He calls me all the way from Germany* (Alemania) *every week.*

_____

11. *Because of his attitude* (la actitud) *and bitterness* (la amargura), *he has no friends.*

_____

12. *The novel* Les Miserables *is by Victor Hugo.*

_____

13. *We are marching* (marchar) *to Pretoria.*

_____

14. *One of them is going to win* (ganar) *the grand prize* (el premio gordo)*!*

_____

15. *I'm tired, and for this reason* (razón) *I'm going to take a nap* (dormir una siesta).

_____

Prepositions of time

Prepositions can be used to indicate a relationship in time, often answering the question *when?* Below are several frequently used prepositions that indicate time.

Me esperarán **hasta** mañana.   *They'll wait for me **until** tomorrow.*
Después de comer, no es bueno dormirse.   ***After** eating, it's not good to fall asleep.*
Llámame **antes de** las ocho.   *Call me **before** eight.*

EJERCICIO
15·7

Underline the correct preposition in parentheses to complete each of the following sentences.

1. Comemos el postre (*dessert*) (antes de | después de) la comida.

2. Hay muchos anuncios (*commercials*) (durante | por) el programa de televisión.

3. En los Estados Unidos, la temporada (*season*) de béisbol es de abril (desde | hasta) octubre.

4. (Antes de | Por) un partido de béisbol, cantamos el himno nacional.

5. Juan ha vivido (*has lived*) en California (por | desde) 2001.

6. Muchas personas trabajan de lunes (a | durante) viernes.

7. Tenemos que lavar los platos (antes de | después de) la cena.

8. No es cortés hablar (antes de | durante) la película.

9. Es importante limpiar la casa (durante | antes de) la fiesta.

10. Muchos consultorios (*offices*) de dentista tocan música (hasta | durante) el día.

11. El senador está en una reunión, pero va a regresar a la oficina (antes de | después de) estar allí.

12. Típicamente, dormimos (por | hasta) la noche.

EJERCICIO
15·8

Traducción *Use the second-person singular Spanish form for English* you.

1. *You don't have to be here until tomorrow.*

   _____

2. *I need to clean the garage before winter.*

   _____

3. *It's cold, isn't it (¿no?)? Yes. Since Tuesday.*

   _____

4. *Some people believe that ghosts* (el fantasma) *live after death* (la muerte).

   _____

5. *After dinner, we always wash the dishes.*

   _____

6. *What do you want to do during our break* (el descanso)?

   _____

7. *Usually, what do you do in the afternoon?*

   _____

8. *What do you want to do before the dance* (el baile)?

   _____

9. *We usually talk during the commercials* (el anuncio).

   _____

10. *He's going to work here until March.*

    _____

11. *Don't you have milk? No. Not since Saturday.*

    _____

12. *They work from Monday to Friday.*

_____

13. *We can watch the movie and go to the restaurant afterwards.*

_____

14. *I always chop* (picar) *the onions before cooking them.*

_____

Prepositions and related adverbs

With many of the compound prepositions that end in **de** (**encima de, cerca de, lejos de**, etc.), especially when the object of the preposition is understood, you drop the **de** in the Spanish sentence when the understood object is omitted. These are most often prepositions indicating location. However, the lack of an object for the preposition converts that preposition into an adverb within the sentence. Both the PREPOSITION + OBJECT and the ADVERB answer the question "*Where?*"

La silla está **cerca de la mesa**.	*The chair is **close to the table**.*
La silla está **cerca**.	*The chair is **close** (nearby).*
La almohada está **encima de la cama**.	*The pillow is **on top of the bed**.*
La almohada está **encima**.	*The pillow is **on the top**.*

Other prepositions indicating location or movement are very closely related to adverbs. The following chart shows six prepositions with related adverbs. The prepositions must be followed by a noun or pronoun as object of the preposition. The adverbs must be placed at the end of a clause or sentence and cannot be followed by a noun.

PREPOSITION		ADVERB	
adelante de	in front of	**hacia adelante**	forward
al lado de	next to	**de lado**	sideways
atrás de	behind	**hacia atrás**	backward
debajo de	below, under	**abajo**	downstairs, underneath
dentro de	inside	**adentro**	inside
fuera de	outside	**afuera**	outside

Ella está **adelante de Miguel** en la cola.	*She is **in front of Miguel** in line.*
Tienes que ir **hacia adelante** en la autopista.	*You must go **forward** on the expressway.*
La silla está **al lado de la mesa**.	*The chair is **next to the table**.*
Un cangrejo camina **de lado**.	*A crab walks **sideways**.*
El acebo está **atrás de la casa**.	*The holly tree is **behind the house**.*
Cuando pones el coche en marcha atrás, tú y el coche van **hacia atrás**.	*When you put the car in reverse, you and the car go **backward**.*
Él está **debajo de la mesa**.	*He is **under the table**.*
Él está **abajo**.	*He is **downstairs**.*
Estamos **dentro de la casa**.	*We are **inside the house**.*
Estamos **adentro**.	*We are **inside**.*
Ellos están **fuera de la casa**.	*They are **outside the house**.*
Ellos están **afuera**.	*They are **outside**.*

Para and Por

Students of Spanish quickly discover that the prepositions **para** and **por** are a force to be reckoned with. At first, we discover that they both mean "for." However, upon closer inspection, we find out that each has several other meanings. Some of those meanings are shared by both prepositions, and others are unique to just one of them.

The issues encountered with **para** and **por** are sometimes compared with those of **ser** and **estar**, both of which translate as English "to be." In the case of **ser** and **estar**, there is one verb in English that corresponds to two verbs in Spanish, each with a list of rules to absorb.

However, an important distinction between these two pairs of words is that **ser** and **estar**, in most grammatical instances, are not interchangeable. When a person makes an error using **ser** or **estar**, that error will register as a mistake in the mind of the listener (the bad news), but the listener will nearly always be able to "fix" the mistake in his or her mind and understand what the speaker intended (the good news).

Para and **por**, on the other hand, are grammatically interchangeable a good deal of the time. You can use one or the other, and you will produce a perfectly well-structured and meaningful sentence (the good news). However, most listeners lack mind-reading skills, and they will therefore assume that you mean what you are actually saying, which may not be the case (the bad news).

Consider the following pair of sentences (their differences will be explained more clearly later in the chapter):

Denyce canta **para** Renée.	*Denyce sings **for** Renée.*
Denyce canta **por** Renée.	*Denyce sings **for** Renée.*

While both sentences translate as "Denyce sings for Renée," they have very different meanings. In the first sentence, Denyce is singing to Renée: Denyce is on the stage, and Renée is sitting happily in the audience listening to the music. In the second sentence, Denyce is singing *on behalf of* Renée: Renée is nowhere to be found, and Denyce takes her place. In this context, Denyce replaces Renée.

In a nutshell, think of **para** as an arrow. In one way or another, **para** tells where something is going. **Por**, on the other hand, is like a balance scale, equalizing what is on both sides of the preposition.

Thus we must be extremely careful in using **para** and **por**. In this chapter, we examine the various meanings of each one in turn: first **para**, then **por**. After working with them individually, we mix them up, as we do in everyday conversation. **Para** and **por**, even though they are just "little words," provide the Spanish speaker with a rich way to describe various relationships of people and things.

Para

Para goes forward, like an arrow, away from its origin toward its destination, and usually in a direct, straight route.

The uses of **para** can be neatly placed into the following four categories: destination, purpose, deadline, and standard. In all four of these categories, which are discussed in detail below, **para** indicates distinguishing qualities of nouns in a sentence, often with movement toward a specific goal or destination.

Para: destination

Para indicates the destination of someone or something, whether that destination is real or imagined. **Para** tells where something is going, could go, or perhaps should go. In this context, **para** nearly always translates as the English "for."

To indicate real or imagined destination

REAL	Este jabón es **para** el baño.	*This soap is **for** the bathroom.* (in the sense of "belongs in")
	Este teléfono es **para** esa oficina.	*This telephone is **for** that office.* (in the sense of "goes into")
IMAGINED	Mi casa es buena **para** la fiesta.	*My house is good **for** the party.*
	Romeo es perfecto **para** Julieta.	*Romeo is perfect **for** Juliet.*

To express the recipient of an action

Para tells not only where, but also *to whom* something is going. The recipient always follows **para**, which translates as English "for" in this context.

Tengo el dinero **para** Juan.	*I have the money **for** John.*
Estos regalos son **para** mí.	*These gifts are **for** me.*

To indicate direction and/or final destination

Para concerns itself only with the final destination, not with any temporary stops along the way. (Contrast this with the use of **por** to indicate an intermediate destination.) In this context, **para** can translate as either English "to" or "for."

Los astronautas van **para** la luna.	*The astronauts go **to** the moon.*
Salimos **para** la iglesia a las nueve.	*We leave **for** church at nine o'clock.*

To indicate an action's aim or objective, including profession

Para is used to indicate the final destination or objective of your studies—or what you want to be. For example, in universities in the United States, students often talk about their major. In Spanish, a student majoring in biology could say, **Estudio *para* médico**, which translates as "I'm studying *to be* a physician," focusing on the final destination. The verb "to be" in this context is understood and therefore can be omitted. You can, if you want, include **ser** ("to be"), as in the sentence **Estudio para *ser* médico**. Note that with this usage, the profession usually remains singular in Spanish, even when the subject is plural, as in the second example below.

Ella estudia **para** electricista.	*She is studying **to be** an electrician.*
Ellos estudian **para** carpintero.	*They are studying **to be** carpenters.*

Para: purpose

To express purpose before an infinitive

Something's purpose is the reason that it exists. In describing what something does, or what it is for, use **para** + VERB. Because a verb is never conjugated after a preposition, the format will always be **para** + INFINITIVE. This use of **para** translates as English "for."

Una pluma estilográfica es **para** escribir.	*A fountain pen is **for** writing.*
Estos zapatos son **para** correr.	*These shoes are **for** running.*

To indicate purpose for doing something; "in order to" before an infinitive

To give the reason for doing something, use **para** + INFINITIVE. In this case, **para** translates as English "to" or "in order to."

Yo como **para** vivir.	*I eat **to** live.*
Estudiamos **para** aprender.	*We study **in order to** learn.*

Para: deadline

To express a specific time limit or deadline in the future

Use **para** to specify a time limit or deadline in the future, for example, to state by when you need a certain action to have been completed. In this context, **para** usually translates as English "by"; however, it can also mean "for," "on," or "no later than."

Tenemos que hacer esto **para** esta noche.	*We have to do this **by** tonight.*
Necesita el vestido **para** el fin de semana.	*She needs the dress **for** the weekend.*
Necesitamos el informe **para** el sábado.	*We need the report **on** Saturday.*
Necesito la ropa **para** el jueves.	*I need the clothes **no later than** Thursday.*

To express a limited time span in the future

Use **para** to express an action that stretches out over a specific period of time in the future. Typically, this is a generalized period of time, as opposed to a period that begins at a specific hour and then ends at a specific hour in the future. This use of **para** translates as English "for."

Él tiene empleo **para** el verano.	*He has work **for** the summer.*
Tenemos una casa reservada **para** dos semanas.	*We have a house reserved **for** two weeks.*

Para: standard

To express a comparison to a certain standard

When comparing someone or something that goes beyond what is expected to what would typically be expected, use **para** to express that comparison. **Para** in these cases translates as the English "for."

Paco es alto **para** su edad.	*Paco is tall **for** his age.*
Hace calor **para** enero.	*It's warm **for** January.*

To express an opinion or personal standard

In order to say, "in my opinion," you can say, literally, **en mi opinión**, or you can say more simply, **para mí**. This construction is used with both names and pronouns. In this context, **para** translates as English "for."

Para mí, el español es hermoso.	***For me**, Spanish is beautiful.*
Para Paco, Portland es la mejor ciudad.	***For Paco**, Portland is the best city.*

Summary

The four categories of the uses of **para** are listed below. Use this list when doing the exercises that follow.

1. Destination
   a. To indicate real or imagined destination
   b. To express the recipient of an action
   c. To indicate direction and/or final destination
   d. To indicate an action's aim or objective, including profession

2. Purpose
   e. To express purpose before an infinitive
   f. To indicate purpose for doing something; "in order to" before an infinitive

3. Deadline
   g. To express a specific time limit or deadline in the future
   h. To express a limited time span in the future

4. Standard
   i. To express a comparison to a certain standard
   j. To express an opinion or personal standard

EJERCICIO 16·1

Write the letter from the preceding summary list that corresponds to the reason for using **para** *in each of the following sentences.*

_____ 1. Tenemos que pagar los impuestos (*taxes*) para el 15 de abril.

_____ 2. Santa Claus sólo tiene carbón para ella.

_____ 3. Pongo la radio para escuchar la música.

_____ 4. Vamos para Amsterdam este verano.

_____ 5. Para una persona inteligente, un presidente debe ser diplomático.

_____ 6. Para recibir buenas notas (*grades*), necesitas trabajar mucho.

_____ 7. Camila toma clases para actriz.

_____ 8. Este jabón es para el cuerpo y ése es para la cara.

_____ 9. ¡Para un restaurante de cuatro estrellas, esta comida está horrible!

_____ 10. Este papel es para envolver regalos.

_____ 11. Para Abby, mirar una película es una buena manera de pasar la noche.

_____ 12. Ellas estudian para bibliotecarias.

_____ 13. Está muy nublado para un día de junio.

_____ 14. Para mí, es muy bueno sacar fotos de ocasiones importantes.

_____ 15. Tienes que hacer algo para tu novia en el día de San Valentín.

_____ 16. Este detergente es para lavar la ropa.

_____ 17. Tengo empleo para el año que viene.

_____ 18. Salimos para la discoteca a la medianoche.

_____ 19. Este espejo (*mirror*) es para la entrada de la casa.

_____ 20. Ella es muy inteligente para una niña de sólo tres años.

EJERCICIO
16·2

Traducción *The words and expressions in* **bold italic** *translate as* **para**. *Unless otherwise indicated, use the second-person singular Spanish form for English* you.

1. *This house is perfect **for** us.*

_____

2. *We need a new table **for** the dining room.*

_____

3. ***For** some people, it isn't important to have a car.*

_____

4. *These shoes are **for** dancing the tango.*

_____

5. *You have to read this book **by** Thursday.*

_____

6. *He watches television **to** avoid* (evitar) *his problems.*

_____

7. *I'm leaving **for** Africa tomorrow.*

_____

8. *I'm studying **to be** a magician* (el mago).

_____

9. *He's very polite* (cortés) ***for** a teenager* (el adolescente).

_____

10. *Can you write the letter **by** Tuesday?*

_____

11. *This food is **for** the cat.*

_____

12. ***For** him, winter is wonderful, but **for** me, summer is the best season* (la estación).

_____

13. *She works a lot **in order to** get (sacar) good grades.*

_____

14. *What time do you leave **for** work (el trabajo)?*

_____

15. *These apples are not **for** eating.*

_____

Por

Like a balance scale, **por** is a great equalizer. The use of **por** indicates a sense of equality about whatever is on either side of **por** in a sentence. We trade one thing for another because items are perceived as equal in value. We say how long something lasts, equating the action of "lasting" with an amount of time. We substitute one person or thing for another because we consider the two persons or items to be of equal competence or value, at least temporarily.

The uses of **por** can be placed neatly into the following six categories: duration, substitution, motivation, movement, emotions, and idioms. In all six of these categories, which are discussed in detail below, **por** serves to equate or combine nouns in a sentence, rather than distinguish the differences between them.

Por: duration

To express duration of time

When expressing duration, that is, telling how long something lasts, use **por**. In this context, **por** translates as English "for."

Cada día trabajamos **por** ocho horas.	*Every day we work **for** eight hours.*
Ellos van de vacaciones **por** dos semanas.	*They go on vacation **for** two weeks.*

To indicate periods of time during the 24-hour day

Por used before **la mañana**, **la tarde**, **la noche**, or **el día** indicates an unspecified amount of time, yet it implies that whatever is taking place lasts a while (as opposed to an extremely short time). In this context, **por** translates as English "for," "at," "during," "on," or "throughout."

Va a Chicago **por** el día.	*He's going to Chicago **for** the day.*
Tenemos clase **por** la noche.	*We have class **at** night.*
Ella va a estudiar **por** la tarde.	*She's going to study **during** the afternoon.*
Ellos van al templo los viernes **por** la noche.	*They go to synagogue **on** Friday nights.*
Voy al dentista el lunes **por** la tarde.	*I'm going to the dentist **on** Monday afternoon.*
Él toma café **por** el día.	*He drinks coffee **throughout** the day.*

To express English use of Latin *per*

To express times per day, minutes per hour, or the percentage of something, use **por** to express the relationship. This use of **por** indicates duration or a portion of a whole, and it corresponds to the English use of Latin *per*.

| Él lee tres libros **por mes**. | *He reads three books **per month**.* |
| El diez **por ciento** no aprobó el examen. | *Ten **percent** didn't pass the exam.* |

Por: substitution or exchange

To indicate an equal exchange or trade

Por implies an equality of the two nouns that it separates. We freely trade or purchase something, because we perceive that what we are giving is equal in value to what we are getting in return. In this context, **por** usually translates as English "for."

| Pagué ocho dólares **por** la pizza. | *I paid eight dollars **for** the pizza.* |
| Juan cambió su manzana **por** una naranja. | *Juan exchanged his apple **for** an orange.* |

To express substitution ("on behalf of," "in place of")

Por indicates equality in a situation where someone or something is substituted for someone or something else. This is seen in the classroom, in the workplace, and in recipes—whenever the original person or ingredient is not available. In these cases, **por** usually translates as English "for," "on behalf of," or "in place of."

Sustituyo margarina **por** mantequilla.	*I substitute margarine **for** butter.*
El vicepresidente habla **por** el presidente.	*The vice-president speaks **on behalf of** the president.*
Roberto trabaja **por** Miguel.	*Roberto works **in place of** Miguel.*

To express thanks and gratitude

To thank someone for something that he or she has done for you, or to express gratitude for a gift, use **por**. This is another example of **por** as an equalizer. This is why we say that we give thanks *for* a kind deed: the thanks balance the act of giving. In this context, **por** usually translates as English "for."

| Gracias **por** las flores. | *Thank you **for** the flowers.* |
| Te doy las gracias **por** tu ayuda. | *I thank you **for** your help.* |

Por: motivation

To indicate "because of" or having done something (**por** + infinitive)

To express the reason for having done something, use **por** + INFINITIVE. This generally translates as "because of" or "due to." The verb that follows **por** must be in the infinitive. Expressed in English, this verb is a gerund (which functions as a noun in the sentence), and it always ends in "-ing."

| **Por ganar** la lotería, ellos son ricos. | ***Due to winning** the lottery, they are rich.* |
| Él no trabaja hoy **por estar** enfermo. | *He's not working today **because of his being** sick.* |

To express a motive for doing something

Por tells why a person does something by expressing a specific motive. In these cases, **por** can translate as either English "for" or "because of."

| Vamos a la tienda **por** mantequilla. | *We're going to the store **for** butter.* |
| Reconstruimos la casa **por** la tormenta. | *We're rebuilding the house **because of** the storm.* |

To express a reason for something (por + NOUN or por + INFINITIVE)

Por expresses the reason for something being the way it is; it expresses "Why?" In these cases, **por** is followed by either a noun or an infinitive. The Spanish verb that follows **por**, when expressed in English, is a gerund (which functions as a noun in the sentence) that always ends in "-ing." **Por** can translate as English "for," "due to," or "because of."

Beethoven es famoso **por su música**.	Beethoven is famous **for his music**.
Soy más fuerte **por tener la experiencia**.	I am stronger **for having the experience**.
Beethoven es famoso **por componer su música**.	Beethoven is famous **for composing his music**.
Paco es popular **por ser tan inteligente**.	Paco is popular **for being so intelligent**.
Ella ahorra mucho dinero **por los cupones**.	She saves a lot of money **due to coupons**.
Ella ahorra mucho dinero **por usar cupones**.	She saves a lot of money **due to using coupons**.
Sara es popular **por su personalidad**.	Sara is popular **because of her personality**.
Soy más fuerte **por la experiencia**.	I am stronger **because of the experience**.

Por: movement

To express means of transportation

To express how someone gets somewhere, use **por** before the mode of transportation. Several common forms of transportation are listed here. This use of **por** translates as English "by" or "on."

por autobús	*by bus*	**por** ferrocarril, **por** tren	*by rail,* *by train*
por avión	*by airplane*	**por** coche/carro	*by car*

Viajan de Londres a París **por tren**.	*They travel from London to Paris* ***by train***.
Martín va al trabajo **por autobús**.	*Martin goes to work* ***on the bus***.

NOTE The preposition **en** is also used in this way: **en avión, en tren**, etc.

To express means of sending messages or information

To talk about sending a message, use the preposition **por**. Several common ways of sending messages or information are listed here. In this context, **por** can translate as English "by," "on," or "via."

por computadora	*by computer*	**por** fax	*by fax*
por correo	*by mail*	**por** teléfono	*by phone,* ***on*** *the telephone*
por correo electrónico	*by e-mail*	**por** texto	*by text*

Le envío un regalo **por correo**.	*I'm sending him a gift* ***by mail***.
No es bueno discutir **por teléfono**.	*It's not good to fight* ***on the telephone***.
Me responde **por e-mail**.	*He responds to me* ***via e-mail***.

To indicate the point of an intermediate destination

To indicate an intermediate destination or a temporary stop, use **por**—for example, a stop by someone's house or a layover that's part of a longer trip. Any temporary stop that is not your final destination is indicated by using **por**. (Contrast this with the use of **para** to indicate final destination.) In this context, **por** translates as English "by" or "through."

Voy **por** el banco antes de ir al teatro.	*I'm going* ***by*** *the bank before going to the theater.*
Pasamos **por** Detroit en el viaje a París.	*We're going* ***through*** *Detroit on the trip to Paris.*

To indicate movement in an area

While **para** indicates movement to or toward a destination, **por** indicates that the person is already there and is moving around in a general, nonspecific direction. In such cases, **por** can translate as English "around," "through," "throughout," or "by."

Nos paseamos **por** la ciudad.	*We walk **around** the city.*
Nos paseamos **por** el parque.	*We stroll **through** the park.*
El detective busca **por** la casa.	*The detective searches **throughout** the house.*
Marta anda **por** la tienda.	*Marta walks **by** the store.*

Por: emotions

To express a like (or dislike) or an emotion for someone or something

To express having or feeling something that is intangible—such as respect—for someone, use **por**. This contrasts with using **para** to express destination for something tangible, such as a book.

Think of it like this: When you give something tangible away, you are left with nothing; your hand is empty. But you cannot give away emotions, because no matter how much love you give to someone, you will still be filled with love. Something that's intangible just gets moved around. In this context, **por** nearly always translates as English "for."

Juan tiene mucho amor **por** su esposa.	*John has a lot of love **for** his wife.*
Tengo respeto **por** mis amigos.	*I have respect **for** my friends.*

Por: idioms

To appear in idiomatic expressions

Por is used in hundreds of idiomatic expressions. In a dictionary of Spanish idiomatic usage, several pages of phrases begin with **por**. Below are several of the more frequently used idiomatic expressions that begin with **por**.

VOCABULARIO

por allí	around there, that way
por aquí	around here, this way
por ejemplo	for example
por eso	therefore
por esto	therefore
por favor	as a favor, please
por fin	at last, finally
por (lo) general	as a rule, generally
por lo menos	at least
por medio de	by means of
por primera vez	for the first time
por separado	separately
por supuesto	of course
por todas partes	everywhere
por todos lados	all over, everywhere, on all sides

Summary

The six categories of the uses of **por** are listed below. Use this list while doing the exercises that follow.

1. Duration
   a. To express duration of time
   b. To indicate periods of time during the 24-hour day
   c. To express English use of Latin *per*

2. Substitution or exchange
   d. To indicate an equal exchange or trade
   e. To express substitution ("on behalf of," "in place of")
   f. To express thanks and gratitude

3. Motivation
   g. To indicate "because of" or having done something (**por** + INFINITIVE)
   h. To express a motive for doing something
   i. To express a reason for something (**por** + NOUN or **por** + INFINITIVE)

4. Movement
   j. To express means of transportation
   k. To express means of sending messages or information
   l. To indicate the point of an intermediate destination
   m. To indicate movement in an area

5. Emotions
   n. To express a like (or dislike) or an emotion for someone or something

6. Idioms
   o. To appear in idiomatic expressions

Write the letter from the preceding summary list that corresponds to the reason for using **por** *in each of the following sentences.*

_____ 1. Ella corre por media hora cada día.

_____ 2. Vamos a Amsterdam por avión.

_____ 3. Caminamos por el centro comercial, pero no compramos nada.

_____ 4. Pagamos cien dólares por la silla.

_____ 5. El coche va a sesenta millas por hora.

_____ 6. La policía buscó por todas partes sin encontrar al ladrón (*thief*).

_____ 7. No tengo ningún sentimiento por ti.

_____ 8. Ella siempre duerme una siesta por la tarde.

_____ 9. Gracias por las manzanas.

_____ 10. Él siempre recibe una "A" por estudiar mucho.

_____ 11. Tengo laringitis. Tienes que hablar por mí.

_____ 12. Voy por tu casa antes de ir al cine.

_____ 13. La casa fue destruida por el terremoto.

_____ 14. Voy al centro comercial por un vestido.

_____ 15. Vamos al teatro el sábado por la noche.

_____ 16. No quiero pagar más de diez dólares por una libra de café.

_____ 17. Ellos siempre compran la comida por separado.

_____ 18. Manejamos por la ciudad en busca del restaurante perfecto.

_____ 19. Puedes enviarme la información por correo electrónico.

_____ 20. Nadie trabaja por mí cuando estoy enfermo.

_____ 21. Voy a la farmacia por medicina.

_____ 22. Ellos prefieren viajar por ferrocarril.

_____ 23. Montaigne es conocido por sus ensayos (_essays_).

_____ 24. Te doy muchas gracias por tu bondad (_kindness_).

_____ 25. Por comprar tantas cosas, ella está sin plata (_broke_).

Traducción _Translate the following sentences into Spanish. The word or phrase to be replaced by_ **por** _or an idiomatic expression with_ **por** _appears in_ **_bold italic_**. _Unless otherwise indicated, use the second-person singular Spanish form for English_ you.

1. _We go to school **by** bus._

   _____

2. _You can have those shoes **for** ten dollars._

   _____

3. _He has **at least** twenty cats._

   _____

4. _When I travel, I always walk **through** the city and I investigate_ (investigar) _everything._

   _____

5. _We read the newspaper **for** thirty minutes every morning._

   _____

6. _Juanita is sick today. Can you work **for** her?_

   _____

7. _I'm going to the supermarket **for** milk, butter, and eggs._

   _____

8. *Every **Monday night** he watches football (el fútbol americano) on television.*

_____

9. ***Because of** her allergies (las alergias), she can't touch the cat.*

_____

10. *Thanks **for** nothing.*

_____

11. ***For** giving so much (tanto) to others, she deserves (merecer) a medal (la medalla).*

_____

12. *Ninety **per**cent of all the dentists say that this toothpaste (la pasta de dientes) is horrible.*

_____

13. *He comes **by** my house now and then (de vez en cuando).*

_____

14. *I only have admiration (la estimación) **for** you.*

_____

15. *I now understand the differences between por and para **for** the first time.*

_____

16. *You can send me the contracts (el contrato) **by** fax.*

_____

*Complete each sentence with the appropriate use of **para** or **por**. Then give the reason for your choice.*

1. Tengo algunas cosas _____ ti.

_____

2. Juan es muy humilde (*modest*) _____ un hombre tan inteligente y rico.

_____

3. Gracias _____ los mapas. Puedo usarlos en mi viaje a España.

_____

4. Cada día Mitch practica el clarinete _____ una hora.

_____

5. Cuando visito un museo, siempre camino _____ todas las galerías.

_____

6. El concierto comienza a las ocho. Quiero llegar al teatro _____ las siete y media.

_____

7. Los juguetes de Mattel son _____ los niños.

_____

8. Yo tomo café _____ la mañana y _____ la tarde, pero nunca _____ la noche.

_____

9. Estas toallas (*towels*) son _____ el baño principal.

_____

10. Batman y Robin siempre viajan _____ Batmobile, y nunca _____ autobús.

_____

11. Este restaurante es demasiado costoso. ¡Cuarenta dólares _____ una ensalada es ridículo!

_____

12. ¿Estás listo (*ready*)? Salimos _____ la biblioteca ahora.

_____

13. Tengo hambre. ¿Hay un restaurante _____ aquí?

_____

14. No hay clases hoy y nada está abierto _____ la nieve.

_____

15. Me abono (*subscribe*) a dos periódicos _____ saber las noticias del mundo.

_____

16. Cuando la actriz principal está enferma, su suplente (*understudy*) se presenta _____ ella.

_____

17. Me cepillo los dientes más o menos cinco veces _____ día.

_____

18. El dentista cree que debemos cepillarnos los dientes _____ lo menos dos veces al día.

_____

19. Martín cree que el sistema métrico es el mejor, pero _____ mí, prefiero pies y pulgadas.

_____

20. Antes de la fiesta, vamos _____ la tienda a comprar unos refrescos.

_____

21. Siento nada menos que (*nothing but*) disgusto _____ ellos.

_____

22. Uso e-mail _____ escribir notas a mis colegas.

_____

23. No tenemos ni luces ni electricidad _____ no pagar la cuenta de utilidades a tiempo.

_____

24. John Phillips Sousa es famoso _____ sus marchas.

_____

25. Cada día hablo con mi esposo _____ teléfono.

_____

26. Después de veinte años, _____ fin Carlota ganó la lotería.

_____

27. Comemos _____ vivir.

_____

28. Vamos a tener una fiesta el sábado _____ la noche.

_____

29. Solamente el treinta _____ ciento de los médicos recomiendan esta medicina.

_____

30. Ustedes tienen que terminar el proyecto _____ finales del mes.

_____

EJERCICIO
16·6

The following eight pairs of sentences differ either very little or not at all, except in the use of **para** and **por**. Translate each sentence into English, and then describe its meaning based on the use of **para** or **por**.

EJEMPLO a. Juan cocina para Juanita.

Juan cooks for Juanita.

Destination: Juanita is in the dining room, awaiting her meal.

b. Juan cocina por Juanita.

Juan cooks for Juanita.

Substitution: Juanita would normally cook the meal, but Juan is doing it for her.

1. a. Puedes tener mi camisa para tu falda.

_____

_____

   b. Puedes tener mi camisa por tu falda.

_____

_____

2. a. Vamos para su casa esta noche.

_____

_____

   b. Vamos por su casa esta noche.

_____

_____

3. a. Tengo muchas muestras (*samples*) de champú y jabón para el viaje.

_____

_____

   b. Tengo muchas muestras de champú y jabón por el viaje.

_____

_____

4. a. Tengo muchos regalos para Daisy y para Lily.

_____

_____

   b. Tengo mucho amor por Daisy y por Lily.

_____

_____

5. a. Maksim baila para Derek.

_____

_____

   b. Maksim baila por Derek.

_____

_____

6. a. Conducimos para el parque.

_____

_____

b. Conducimos por el parque.

_____

_____

7. a. Estas cremas son para las alergias.

_____

_____

b. Estas alergias son por las cremas.

_____

_____

8. a. Para mí, esta sopa está mala.

_____

_____

b. Por mí, esta sopa está mala.

_____

_____

Traducción

VOCABULARIO	la erradicación	eradication
	la buena noticia (es)	the good news (is)
	la vacuna	vaccine
	afectar	to affect
	la pandemia	pandemic
	el acrónimo (de)	acronym (for)
	el síntoma	symptom
	el resfrió fuerte	bad cold
	la gripe	flu
	la fiebre	fever
	la tos	cough
	la tasa de mortalidad más baja	lowest death rate
	la mialgia	myalgia
	la fatiga	fatigue
	los casos graves	severe cases
	caracterizarse (por)	to be characterized (por)
	la neumonía	pneumonia
	respirar	to breathe
	han muerto	have died (3rd person pl.)
	en todo el mundo	all over the world
	continuar propagándose	to continue to spread
	el peor récord	the worst record
	el cuarto	quarter
	sin un final a la vista	with no end in sight

This is a situation that affects everyone: the pandemic novel-Coronavirus, or COVID-19, an acronym for coronavirus-19. It produces symptoms similar to those such as a cold or influenza, and includes fever, cough, myalgia, and fatigue. In serious cases it is characterized by pneumonia, difficulty in breathing, sepsis and septic shock. More than two million people have died worldwide, and it continues to spread. The country with the worst record of management of COVID-19 is the United States where more than a half a million people have died, with no end in sight. The countries with the best responses to the pandemic, and thus the lowest death rates, include Taiwan, Singapore, and New Zealand. In each of these countries, the leaders have taken the pandemic seriously and mandated precautions that include the use of facemasks in public, avoiding crowds, maintaining social distance and washing one's hands. While these are simple things, some people believe they are difficult and unnecessary. But nothing is more difficult than death. The good news is that there are now vaccines that protect people, and that the new President, Joe Biden, considers the eradication of COVID-19 his number one priority.

Prepositions and Verbs

The relationship between prepositions and verbs is a special one. In some cases, the preposition exists within the definition of the verb itself. In other cases, the meaning of the verb depends on the preposition that follows it. In this chapter, your vocabulary will expand significantly as you explore the intricate relationship that often exists between prepositions and verbs.

Verbs whose meanings include a preposition

There are many Spanish verbs whose definitions in English include a preposition. It is important to know these verbs in order to resist the temptation to add a preposition in Spanish when none is needed or adding one is grammatically incorrect.

Busco mis zapatos.	*I'm looking for* my shoes.
Miras las pinturas.	*You look at* the paintings.
Los trapos **empapan** el aceite.	*The rags* **soak up** *the oil.*
El jardinero **arranca** la maleza.	*The gardener* **pulls out** *the weeds.*
Escuchamos música.	*We listen to* music.
Encendemos las luces.	*We turn on* the lights.
Apagamos las luces.	*We turn off* the lights. OR
	We turn out the lights.

Below are frequently used Spanish verbs whose definitions in English include a preposition. The understood preposition is *italicized* in the definition.

VOCABULARIO

agradecer	to be grateful/thankful *for*
anhelar	to yearn/long *to*
apagar	to turn *off*
aprobar (o > ue)	to approve *of*
arrancar	to root *up*, to pull *out*, to turn *on* (an engine)
atravesar (e > ie)	to go/run *through*, to go *across*
averiguar	to find *out*
bajar	to go *down*
borrar	to cross *out*
botar	to throw *away*, to toss *out*

buscar	to look *for*
caerse	to fall *down*
calentar (e > ie)	to heat/warm *up*
colgar (o > ue)	to hang *up*
conocer	to be acquainted *with*
cortar	to cut *off*, to cut *out*
criar	to bring *up* ("to rear," "to raise")
derribar	to knock *down*, to tear *down*
destacar	to stand *out*
empapar	to soak/sponge *up*
encender (e > ie)	to turn *on* (lights)
enseñar	to point *out*
entregar	to hand *over*
envolver (o > ue)	to wrap *up*
escuchar	to listen *to*
esperar	to wait *for*, to hope *for*
huir	to flee/escape *from*, to run *away*
ignorar	to be ignorant/unaware *of*
indicar	to point *out*
llevarse	to take *out*, to take *away*
lograr	to succeed *in*, to manage *to*
mirar	to look *at*
organizar	to organize, to set *up*
pagar	to pay *for*
pedir (e > i)	to ask *for*
pisar	to step *on*
platicar	to talk *over*
poder (o > ue)	to be able *to*
poner	to turn *on* (an appliance)
pretender	to seek/aspire *to*, to claim *to*
quitar	to take *off*
recoger	to pick *up*
rogar (o > ue)	to beg *for*, to pray *for*
saber	to know how *to* (do something)
sacar	to take *out*
salir	to go *out* (of a place, on a date)
señalar	to point *out*
separar	to set *apart*
soler (o > ue)	to be accustomed *to*, to be in the habit *of*
soplar	to blow *out*
subir	to go *up*, to come *up*, to get *on* (a train, bus, etc.)
tachar	to cross *out*
tender (e > ie)	to hang *out* (laundry), to spread *out*
yacer	to lie *down*

NOTE Some of these verbs have additional definitions that do not include a preposition in English.

EJERCICIO

¿Verdadero o falso?

_____ 1. Usualmente, yo como en un restaurante, pero a veces me llevo la comida.

_____ 2. Antes de preparar la carne, siempre quito la grasa (*fat*).

_____ 3. Vanna White señala las letras en el popular programa *La Rueda de la Fortuna*.

_____ 4. Cada sábado por la noche yo salgo con otra estrella de cine.

_____ 5. El trabajo del detective con frecuencia es averiguar quién es el asesino (*murderer*).

_____ 6. El gallo atraviesa la calle para llegar al otro lado.

_____ 7. Me encanta soplar las velitas (*candles*) en la torta (*cake*) de cumpleaños.

_____ 8. Cada día quito el polvo (*dust*) en mi casa o apartamento.

_____ 9. Yo sé bailar el merengue.

_____ 10. Yo merezco ganar la lotería.

_____ 11. Cuelgo el teléfono cuando me llama un vendedor a quien no conozco.

_____ 12. Las personas que vuelan en primera clase suben antes que los pasajeros en la clase turista.

_____ 13. Siempre pongo la radio cuando conduzco (*drive*) largas distancias.

_____ 14. Yo suelo estudiar por la noche y trabajar por el día.

_____ 15. Apago las luces cuando miro la televisión.

_____ 16. Mozart destaca por su música.

EJERCICIO
17·1

Traducción *Translate the following sentences into Spanish, using the list of verbs on pages 149–150.*

1. *I am grateful for everything.*

_____

2. *What are you looking for? I'm looking for my glasses* (los anteojos).

_____

3. *Where should we hang up our coats* (el abrigo)?

_____

4. *I like to listen to classical music* (la música clásica).

_____

5. *You can turn off the lights because we're going to bed now.*

_____

6. *The babysitter* (la niñera) *picks up the toys* (el juguete).

_____

7. *He crosses out all his mistakes* (el error).

_____

8. *Tonight Carlota is going to go out with Guillermo. She is very excited* (ilusionado).

_____

9. *I always take out the garbage* (la basura). *You should take out the garbage once in a while* (de vez en cuando).

_____

10. *The lawyer hands over the evidence* (la evidencia) *to the judge* (el juez).

_____

11. *The rags* (el trapo) *soak up the oil* (el aceite).

_____

12. *The driver* (el conductor) *steps on the brake* (el freno).

_____

13. *I need more money. I'm going to ask for a raise* (el aumento) *tomorrow.*

_____

14. *How long* (¿Por cuánto tiempo?) *do we have to wait for the bus?*

_____

15. *You can turn on the lights here and turn off the lights over there* (allá).

_____

Verbs that follow prepositions

When a verb immediately follows a preposition, it *always* remains in the infinitive form. There is no exception to this rule. Usually the English translation of the infinitive will be in the gerund, or "-ing" form. However, at times the verb may translate as the infinitive in English as well.

Antes de comer, me lavo las manos.
Before eating, I wash my hands.

Después de comer, lavo los platos.
After eating, I wash the dishes.

En vez de estudiar, voy a dormir.
Instead of studying, I'm going to sleep.

Además de andar, puedo masticar chicle.
In addition to walking, I can chew gum.

Pienso **en conseguir** un gato.
I am thinking of getting a cat.

Para recibir una "A," necesitas trabajar duro.
In order to receive an "A," you need to work hard.

¿Verdadero o falso?

_____ 1. Además de tocar la guitarra, Bruce Springsteen también canta.

_____ 2. Antes de comprar un libro, normalmente leo uno o dos capítulos en la librería.

_____ 3. A veces, en vez de cepillarme los dientes, mastico chicle.

_____ 4. Después de ganar las elecciones, el nuevo presidente siempre cumple (*keeps*) las promesas.

_____ 5. Además de tomar esta clase de español, voy a tomar por lo menos (*at least*) dos clases adicionales.

_____ 6. Para mantener bien un coche, se necesita cambiar el aceite cada tres meses.

_____ 7. Después de ganar la Serie Mundial, los jugadores van directamente a Disney World.

_____ 8. Pienso en comprar un coche nuevo.

_____ 9. Normalmente me ducho antes de acostarme.

_____ 10. Pienso en renunciar a (*quitting*) mi trabajo.

_____ 11. Para estar a la moda, es necesario gastar (*spend*) muchísimo dinero por la ropa.

_____ 12. Este año, en lugar de cortar (*mow*) el césped (*lawn*), voy a comprar una cabra (*goat*).

Traducción

1. *We're going to drive to Vermont instead of flying.*

   _____

2. *Before buying the eggs, you should look inside the carton* (el cartón).

   _____

3. *I always feel better after exercising* (hacer ejercicio).

   _____

4. *Besides being able to fly, Superman can see through* (a través de) *walls* (la pared).

   _____

5. *I'm thinking about writing a novel.*

   _____

6. *In order to get* (llegar) *to the bank, you should turn* (doblar) *right on Park Avenue.*

   _____

7. *Do you want to swim instead of playing golf?*

_____

8. *She always eats a protein bar* (la barra de proteína) *after swimming.*

_____

9. *What do you have to do before leaving?*

_____

10. *I'm going to a lecture* (la conferencia) *about using computers.*

_____

11. *In addition to boiling* (hervir) *water, this stove* (la estufa) *can boil milk!*

_____

12. *John has to take three more classes in order to graduate* (graduarse).

_____

Verbs that require a preposition

Many Spanish verbs require a preposition before the following word for a specific usage. That word is typically a noun or the infinitive form of another verb. For the most part, these verbs and their respective prepositions must be learned as one would learn other vocabulary words.

Below are several of these verbs, grouped by preposition and arranged alphabetically within groups. Following each VERB + PREPOSITION is the abbreviation for the part of speech that usually follows the verb in this usage, the verb's English equivalent, and an indicator of the usage itself. For example, the entry "**cuidar a** (*n.*), to take care of (someone)" could be illustrated by this example: **Yo cuido a Juan** ("I take care of Juan"). The entry, "**acabar de** (*v.*), to have just (done something)," gives you enough information to write **María acaba de escribir una carta** ("María has just written a letter").

NOTE In the entries for verbs listed under **a**, remember that the **a** following these verbs is a preposition. Be careful not to confuse the preposition **a** with the personal **a** (which is placed after verbs when the stated direct object is a person).

Abbreviations include (*v.*) for *verb* and (*n.*) for *noun*.

a

Verbs that are followed by **a** are often referred to as "springboard verbs" because they mark the beginning of an action. As you look through the following list of verbs, you will find that many of them move toward an action or lead a person ahead, either literally or figuratively.

Remember that the preposition **a** means "to," and that when you go *to* something, you are moving ahead, going forward.

acertar a (*v.*)	to manage to (*do something*), to succeed in (*doing something*)
acostumbrarse a (*n./v.*)	to become used to (*someone/something*), to become used to (*doing something*)
adaptarse a (*n./v.*)	to adapt oneself to (*something* [*a situation*] / *doing something*)
adelantarse a (*n./v.*)	to step forward to (*someone/something / doing something*)

animar a (*v.*)	to encourage to (*do something*)
animarse a (*v.*)	to decide to (*do something*), to make up one's mind to (*do something*)
aprender a (*v.*)	to learn to (*do something*)
apresurarse a (*n./v.*)	to hasten to (*somewhere / do something*), to hurry to (*somewhere / do something*)
arriesgarse a (*v.*)	to risk (*doing something*)
asistir a (*n.*)	to attend (*something [a function]*)
asomarse a (*n.*)	to appear at (*something*), to look out from (*something*)
aspirar a (*v.*)	to aspire to (*do something / be someone*)
atreverse a (*v.*)	to dare to (*do something*)
aventurarse a (*v.*)	to venture to (*do something*)
ayudar a (*v.*)	to help to (*do something*), to aid in (*doing something*)
burlar a (*n.*)	to deceive (*someone*), to play a trick on (*someone*)
comenzar a (*v.*)	to begin to (*do something*)
comprometerse a (*v.*)	to make a commitment to (*do something*)
condenar a (*v.*)	to condemn to (*do something*)
consagrarse a (*n.*)	to devote oneself to (*someone/something*)
contribuir a (*n./v.*)	to contribute to (*something / doing something*)
convidar a (*n./v.*)	to invite to (*something [a function] / do something*)
correr a (*n./v.*)	to run to (*somewhere / do something*)
cuidar a (*n.*)	to care for (*someone [a person, a pet]*), to take care of (*someone [a person, a pet]*)
dar a (*n.*)	to face (*something*)
dar cuerda a (*n.*)	to wind (*something [a watch]*)
decidirse a (*v.*)	to decide to (*do something*)
dirigirse a (*n./v.*)	to go to (*somewhere*), to address (*someone*), to direct oneself to (*doing something*)
disponerse a (*v.*)	to prepare to (*do something*), to be disposed to (*do something*)
empezar a (*v.*)	to begin to (*do something*)
enseñar a (*v.*)	to teach to (*do something*)
forzar a (*v.*)	to force to (*do something*)
impulsar a (*v.*)	to impel to (*do something*)
incitar a (*v.*)	to incite to (*do something*)
inducir a (*v.*)	to induce to (*do something*)
inspirar a (*v.*)	to inspire to (*do something*)
instar a (*v.*)	to urge to (*do something*)
invitar a (*v.*)	to invite to (*do something*)
ir a (*n./v.*)	to go to (*somewhere*), to be going to (*do something*)
limitarse a (*v.*)	to limit oneself to (*doing something*)
llegar a (*n./v.*)	to arrive at (*somewhere*) / to be going to (*do something*)
meterse a (*v.*)	to take up (*doing something*)
montar a (*n.*)	to ride (*something [a horse]*)
negarse a (*v.*)	to refuse to (*do something*)
obligar a (*v.*)	to oblige to (*do something*), to force to (*do something*)
ofrecerse a (*v.*)	to offer to (*do something*), to promise to (*do something*), to volunteer to (*do something*)
oler a (*n.*)	to smell like (*something*)
oponerse a (*n./v.*)	to oppose (*something / doing something*), to be in opposition to (*something / doing something*)
pararse a (*v.*)	to stop to (*do something*)
parecerse a (*n.*)	to resemble (*someone/something*)
pasar a (*n./v.*)	to pass to (*something / doing something*), to proceed to (*something / doing something*)

persuadir a (*v.*)	to persuade to (*do something*)
ponerse a (*v.*)	to begin to (*do something*), to set out to (*do something*)
prestarse a (*v.*)	to lend oneself to (*doing something*)
probar a (*v.*)	to try to (*do something*), to attempt to (*do something*)
quedarse a (*v.*)	to stay to (*do something*), to remain to (*do something*)
rebajarse a (*n./v.*)	to stoop to (*something* [*a situation*] */ doing something*)
reducirse a (*n./v.*)	to reduce *a situation* or oneself to (*something / doing something*)
rehusar a (*v.*)	to refuse to (*do something*)
renunciar a (*n.*)	to renounce (*something*), to give up (*something*), to quit (*something* [*a job*])
resignarse a (*n./v.*)	to resign oneself to (*something / doing something*)
resistirse a (*n./v.*)	to resist (*something / doing something*)
resolverse a (*v.*)	to make up one's mind to (*do something*), to resolve to (*do something*)
retirarse a (*n./v.*)	to retire to (*somewhere / do something*)
romper a (*v.*)	to start suddenly to (*do something*)
saber a (*n.*)	to taste like (*something*)
sentarse a (*n./v.*)	to sit down to (*something / do something*)
someterse a (*n./v.*)	to submit oneself to (*something / doing something*)
sonar a (*n.*)	to sound like (*something*)
subir a (*n.*)	to go up to (*something*), to climb (*something*), to get on (*something*)
venir a (*n./v.*)	to come to (*somewhere / do something*)
volver a (*n./v.*)	to return to (*somewhere*), to (*do something*) again

◆ **EJERCICIO**

¿Verdadero o falso?

_____ 1. Doy cuerda a mi reloj cada día.

_____ 2. Me niego a volar cuando está lloviendo.

_____ 3. Yo creo que el pavo sabe a pollo.

_____ 4. Nadie puede forzarme a hacer nada.

_____ 5. Siempre rompo a llorar en una boda.

_____ 6. Quiero renunciar a mi trabajo.

_____ 7. Después de sentarme a comer, rehúso a contestar el teléfono.

_____ 8. Nunca me rebajo a robar dulces de un niño.

_____ 9. Nadie puede persuadirme a comer una carpa dorada (*goldfish*), ni por un millón de dólares.

_____ 10. Me parezco a uno de mis primos.

_____ 11. Peter Jennings se parece a James Bond.

_____ 12. A veces el ronroneo (*purring*) de un gato suena a un barco de motor.

_____ 13. La memoria de la madre Teresa me inspira a ser una mejor persona.

_____ 14. Mi casa da al este.

_____ 15. Cuando subo a mi coche, me pongo el cinturón de seguridad inmediatamente.

EJERCICIO

17·3

Traducción *Translate the following sentences into Spanish, using the preceding list of verbs that require* **a.**

1. *This sounds like a lie to me.*

   _____

2. *She bursts out crying* (llorar) *every time she remembers the pain* (el dolor) *of her childhood* (la niñez).

   _____

3. *He's going to quit his job, because his company* (la compañía) *is going to begin to downsize* (recortar el personal).

   _____

4. *Sooner or later* (tarde o temprano), *you have to resign yourself to the fact* (el hecho de) *that some people are not honest* (honrado).

   _____

5. *You can't force us to do anything that we don't want to do.*

   _____

6. *Benjamín winds his watch every day at nine o'clock in the morning.*

   _____

7. *Mrs. Dalí encourages her children to study the fine arts* (las bellas artes).

   _____

8. *In this house, we sit down to eat dinner* (cenar) *at seven o'clock sharp* (en punto).

   _____

9. *What time do we get on the train?*

   _____

10. *This frog tastes like a toad* (el sapo).

    _____

11. *Mateo says that snake meat* (la carne de culebra) *tastes like chicken.*

    _____

12. *Oscar Wilde says that he can resist everything but* (salvo) *temptation* (la tentación).

    _____

13. *In this section of the book, we learn how to use verbs that take* (tomar) *the preposition* a.

    _____

14. *Some athletes* (el atleta) *become used to receiving and spending* (gastar) *lots of money.*

    _____

15. *Richard is not disposed to giving us anything today. He is not in the mood* (de humor).

    _____

Prepositions and Verbs   **157**

con

Verbs that require the preposition **con** sometimes clearly have the meaning "with," as in **asociarse con**, which means "to associate with." For other verbs, it takes deciphering the real meaning of the verb to understand more clearly why it takes **con**.

For example, the verb **casarse con**, which means "to marry," has as its root the noun **la casa** ("house"). The verb **casarse con** actually means "to set up a house for oneself with (*someone*)." Another frequently used verb, **encontrarse con** ("to run into," "to meet up with"), means literally, "to find oneself with."

aburrirse con (*n.*)	to be bored with (*someone/something*), to get bored with (*someone/something*)
acabar con (*n.*)	to finish with/off (*someone/something*), to get rid of (*someone/something*)
amenazar con (*n./v.*)	to threaten with (*something / doing something*)
asociarse con (*n.*)	to associate with (*someone*), to team up with (*someone*)
asustarse con (*n.*)	to be afraid of (*someone/something*), to be frightened by (*someone/something*)
bastarle a alguien con (*n./v.*)	to have enough of (*something / doing something*)
casarse con (*n.*)	to marry (*someone*)
comerciar con (*n.*)	to trade with (*someone/something* [*a business*]), to trade in (*something* [*a business*])
conformarse con (*n./v.*)	conform to (*something / doing something*), to resign oneself to (*something / doing something*), to make do with (*something / doing something*)
contar con (*n.*)	to count on (*someone/something*)
contentarse con (*n.*)	to content oneself with (*something*)
dar con (*n.*)	to come upon (*someone/something*)
disfrutar con (*n.*)	to enjoy (*someone/something*)
divertirse con (*n.*)	to enjoy (*someone/something*), to have fun with (*someone/something*), to have a good time with (*someone/something*)
encontrarse con (*n.*)	to meet up with (*someone*), to run into (*someone*)
enfadarse con (*n.*)	to get angry at/with (*someone/something*)
enojarse con (*n.*)	to get angry at/with (*someone/something*)
equivocarse con (*n.*)	to make a mistake about (*someone/something*), to be mistaken about (*someone/something*)
espantarse con (*n.*)	to become afraid of (*someone/something*)
juntarse con (*n.*)	to associate with (*someone*), to join with (*someone*)
limpiar con (*n.*)	to clean with (*something*)
llenar con (*n.*)	to fill with (*something*)
meterse con (*n.*)	to bother (*someone/something*), to pick a fight with (*someone/something*)
preocuparse con (*n.*)	to worry about (*someone/something*)
recrearse con (*n.*)	to amuse oneself with (*something*)
romper con (*n.*)	to break up with (*someone*), to break off relations with (*someone*)
salir con (*n.*)	to go out with (*someone*), date (*someone*)
soñar con (*n./v.*)	to dream of/about (*someone/something / doing something*)
tratarse con (*n.*)	to associate with (*someone*), to have dealings with (*someone/something*)
tropezarse con (*n.*)	to bump into (*someone/something*), to stumble over (*something*)

¿Verdadero o falso?

_____ 1. A veces me encuentro con amigos para tomar un café.

_____ 2. Disfruto mucho con la música de Lady Gaga.

_____ 3. Un día quiero casarme con alguien de Hollywood.

_____ 4. Me enojo con personas que no me dicen la verdad.

_____ 5. Cuando una persona me miente, generalmente rompo con él o con ella.

_____ 6. Por las mañanas me basta con tomar café.

_____ 7. Sueño con ser una estrella de cine algún día.

_____ 8. Siempre puedo contar con mi mejor amigo/amiga.

_____ 9. Me junto con muchos músicos.

_____ 10. No me asocio con vendedores de drogas ni de pistolas.

_____ 11. Me aburro con la mayoría de los programas en la televisión.

_____ 12. Cuando no hay luces, a veces me tropiezo con el sofá.

_____ 13. Cuando estoy enojado/enojada, amenazo con matar a alguien.

_____ 14. Muchas compañías de los Estados Unidos comercian con Japón.

_____ 15. Siempre me conformo con pagar los impuestos sin quejarme.

Traducción *Translate the following sentences into Spanish, using the preceding list of verbs that require* **con.**

1. *You can count on me, but can I count on you?*

_____

2. *Every Wednesday, I meet up with Kay (in order) to eat dinner* (cenar) *and to converse.*

_____

3. *In the movie* Spiderman, *Peter Parker (Spiderman) dates Mary Jane Watson.*

_____

4. *I become afraid of the dark* (la oscuridad) *during a storm* (la tormenta).

_____

5. *It's tragic, but sometimes* (a veces) *a person needs to break off relations with his/her family.*

_____

6. *The egomaniac* (el egoísta) *dreams of being famous, popular, rich, and powerful* (poderoso).

   _____

7. *I don't associate with companies that sell tobacco* (el tabaco).

   _____

8. *Now and then* (de vez en cuando) *I am mistaken about people* (la persona).

   _____

9. *We always have a good time with our neighbors* (el vecino).

   _____

10. *She gets angry at me when I am late* (llegar tarde).

    _____

11. *Donna has no dealings with her husband's family because they are horrible people.*

    _____

12. *If you clean the bathtub* (la bañera) *with acid* (el ácido), *you're going to damage* (dañar) *it.*

    _____

13. *Now and then I come upon someone who truly* (verdaderamente) *inspires* (inspirar) *me.*

    _____

14. *If Juan isn't careful* (no tener cuidado), *he's going to bump into the wall.*

    _____

15. *On Sunday mornings, I often content myself with orange juice and the newspaper.*

    _____

de

Verbs that are followed by **de** are often verbs of cessation or withdrawal. This is seen clearly in **terminar de** + VERB, which means "to finish (doing something)." The concept of something ending is seen frequently in an examination of the list of verbs below.

The preposition **de** also follows many verbs of emotion. **Aburrirse de** ("to be bored by/with"), **cansarse de** ("to be/get tired of"), **sorprenderse de** ("to be surprised at") are a few examples of verbs of emotion that take **de**.

aburrirse de (*n./v.*)	to be bored by/with (*someone/something / doing something*)
abusar de (*n.*)	to take advantage of (*someone/something*), to impose upon (*someone/something*), to abuse (*someone/something*)
acabar de (*v.*)	to have just (*done something*)
acordarse de (*n./v.*)	to remember (*someone/something*), to remember to (*do something*)
alegrarse de (*n./v.*)	to be glad of/about (*something*), to be happy to (*do something*)
alejarse de (*n.*)	to go/get away from (*someone/something/somewhere*)
aprovecharse de (*n./v.*)	to take advantage of (*someone/something / doing something*)

arrepentirse de (*n./v.*)	to repent for (*something / doing something*), to be sorry for (*something / doing something*)
asombrarse de (*n.*)	to be astonished at (*something*)
avergonzarse de (*n.*)	to be ashamed of (*someone/something*)
brindar a la salud de (*n.*)	to toast (*someone*)
burlarse de (*n.*)	to make fun of (*someone/something*)
cansarse de (*n./v.*)	to be/get tired of (*someone/something / doing something*)
carecer de (*n./v.*)	to lack (*something*)
cesar de (*v.*)	to cease (*doing something*)
conseguir algo de (*n.*)	to obtain/get *something* from (*someone/something*)
cuidar de (*n.*)	to care for (*something*), to take care of (*something*)
deber de (*v.*)	to suppose [*conjecture*] to be (*someone/something*), "must be" (*someone/something*)
dejar de (*v.*)	to stop (*doing something*)
depender de (*n./v.*)	to depend on (*someone/something / doing something*)
encargarse de (*n./v.*)	to take charge of (*someone/something / doing something*)
estar encargado de (*n./v.*)	to be in charge of (*someone/something / doing something*)
gozar de (*n.*)	to enjoy (*something*)
haber de (*v.*)	to suppose [*conjecture*] to (*be/do something*)
hablar de (*n./v.*)	to talk of/about (*someone/something / doing something*), to speak of (*someone/something / doing something*)
jactarse de (*n./v.*)	to brag about (*something / doing something*), to boast of (*something / doing something*)
librarse de (*n.*)	to get rid of (*someone/something*)
llenar(se) de (*n.*)	to fill (up) with (*something*)
maldecir de (*n.*)	to speak ill of (*something*)
maravillarse de (*n.*)	to marvel at (*someone/something*)
marcharse de (*n.*)	to leave (*somewhere*), to walk away from (*somewhere*)
morir de (*n.*)	to die of/from (*something* [*an illness, a situation*])
morirse de (*n.*)	to be dying for/of (*something*)
ocuparse de (*n./v.*)	to concern oneself with (*someone/something / doing something*), to pay attention to (*someone/something / doing something*), to deal with (*someone/something / doing something*)
olvidarse de (*n./v.*)	to forget (*someone/something*), to forget to (*do something*)
parar de (*v.*)	to cease (*doing something*), to stop (*doing something*)
pensar de (*n.*)	to think of (*someone/something*), to have an opinion about (*someone/something*)
preciarse de (*n./v.*)	to brag about (*something / doing something*), to boast of (*something / doing something*), to pride oneself on (*something / doing something*)
prescindir de (*n./v.*)	to do without (*someone/something / doing something*), to neglect (*someone/something / doing something*)
probar de (*n.*)	to sample (*something*), to take a taste of (*something*)
quejarse de (*n./v.*)	to complain of/about (*someone/something / doing something*)
salir de (*n.*)	to leave (*somewhere*), to go away from (*somewhere*)
separarse de (*n.*)	to leave (*someone/something/somewhere*), to part company with (*someone/something/somewhere*)
servir de (*n.*)	to act as (*someone/something*), to serve as (*someone/something*), to be useful for (*someone/something*)
sorprenderse de (*n.*)	to be surprised at (*something*), to be amazed at (*something*)
terminar de (*v.*)	to finish (*doing something*)
tratar de (*v.*)	to try to (*do something*)
tratarse de (*n./v.*)	to be a question of (*something / doing something*)

¿Verdadero o falso?

_____ 1. Acabo de comer un pedazo de pizza.

_____ 2. Usualmente, me alegro de tomar un examen.

_____ 3. Cada primavera me libro de muchas cosas que ya no necesito en mi casa.

_____ 4. Gozo mucho del teatro.

_____ 5. En mi casa estoy encargado/encargada de sacar la basura.

_____ 6. Parte de mi decisión de ir de vacaciones depende de la cantidad de dinero que tengo en el banco.

_____ 7. Me aburro mucho de las personas que no piensan antes de hablar.

_____ 8. Cada día trato de ser una persona honrada (*honest*).

_____ 9. Típicamente salgo de mi casa entre las siete y las nueve de la mañana.

_____ 10. Normalmente no me acuerdo de pagar las cuentas (*bills*) cada mes.

_____ 11. La fruta puede servir de ensalada o de postre.

_____ 12. A veces me olvido del nombre de una persona a quien acabo de conocer.

_____ 13. Cada año miles de personas mueren de cáncer de pulmón (*lung*).

_____ 14. Si no desayuno, para las once de la mañana me muero de hambre.

_____ 15. Muchas personas se quejan de pagar los impuestos cada 15 de abril.

Traducción *Translate the following sentences into Spanish, using the preceding list of verbs that require* **de**.

1. *He always forgets to take his medicine.*

_____

2. *This sofa serves as a comfortable (cómodo) bed.*

_____

3. *We have to finish cleaning the house by four thirty.*

_____

4. *Every day I get rid of at least (por lo menos) five things because I don't like clutter (el desorden).*

_____

5. *She always complains about working so much (tanto).*

_____

6. *I marvel at people who can dance well.*

_____

7. *I'm in charge of cooking, and you're in charge of serving the meals.*

_____

8. *I often forget a person's name, but I never forget the face.*

_____

9. *You should get away from dangerous people.*

_____

10. *I have just read a wonderful article* (el artículo) *in the newspaper.*

_____

11. *Don't we have orange juice? I'm dying of thirst* (la sed).

_____

12. *Who's going to take care of your house next week?*

_____

13. *They're talking about moving* (mudarse) *to Troy, New York, next year.*

_____

14. *I don't like to be with him because he always speaks ill* (mal) *of other people.*

_____

15. *There are people who take advantage of others without remorse* (remordimiento). *They are called social predators* (depredadores sociales).

_____

en

When a Spanish verb takes the preposition **en**, that **en** will often translate as English "in" or "on." For example, **confiar en** means "to confide in, trust"; **insistir en** means "to insist on."

One of the more frequently used verbs in this category is **pensar en**, which usually means "to think about"; however, some English speakers use the expression "to think on." Although some verbs in this category are idiomatic in their translation, many demonstrate the use of "in" or "on." Familiarize yourself with them, and use them until you feel comfortable.

abdicar en (*n.*)	to abdicate to (*someone*)
complacerse en (*n./v.*)	to take pleasure in (*something / doing something*)
confiar en (*n./v.*)	to trust (*someone/something [a situation] / doing something*), to confide in (*someone/something [a situation] / doing something*)
consentir en (*v.*)	to consent to (*do something*)
consistir en (*n./v.*)	to consist of (*something / doing something*)
convenir en (*n./v.*)	to agree to (*something / do something*)
convertirse en (*n.*)	to become (*someone/something*), to change into (*someone/something*)
empeñarse en (*n./v.*)	to insist on (*something / doing something*), to persist in (*something / doing something*), to get involved in (*something / doing something*)

equivocarse en (*n.*)	to make a mistake in (*something*)
esforzarse en (*n./v.*)	to try hard in (*something*), to endeavor to (*do something*)
influir en (*n.*)	to influence (*someone/something*), to have an effect on (*someone/something*)
insistir en (*n./v.*)	to insist on (*something / doing something*)
interesarse en (*n.*)	to be interested in (*someone/something*)
meterse en (*n./v.*)	to become involved in (*something / doing something*)
mojarse en (*n.*)	to get mixed up in (*something*)
molestarse en (*v.*)	to take the trouble to (*do something*)
montar en (*n.*)	to ride (*something [a bicycle]*)
obstinarse en (*n./v.*)	to persist in (*something / doing something*)
ocuparse en (*n./v.*)	to be busy with (*something / doing something*)
parar(se) en (*n.*)	to stop at (*somewhere*), to stay at (*somewhere*)
pensar en (*n./v.*)	to think about (*someone/something / doing something*)
persistir en (*n./v.*)	to persist in (*something / doing something*)
quedar en (*n./v.*)	to agree to (*something / do something*)
reflexionar en (*n.*)	to reflect on (*something*), to think about (*something*)
tardar en (*n./v.*)	to delay in (*something*), to take long to (*do something*)
trabajar en (*n.*)	to work on/at (*something*)
verse en (*n.*)	to find oneself in/at (*something [a situation] / somewhere*)

EJERCICIO

¿Verdadero o falso?

_____ 1. No me gusta meterme en los problemas de los demás.

_____ 2. Los huevos rancheros consiste en huevos y rancheros.

_____ 3. Yo confío en mi mejor amigo/amiga.

_____ 4. En el cuento "Cenicienta," los ratones se convierten en caballos.

_____ 5. La memoria de la madre Teresa influye en muchas personas por el mundo.

_____ 6. Tardo más de veinte minutos en ir de mi casa al aeropuerto.

_____ 7. Es descortés persistir en discutir algo que la otra persona no quiere discutir.

_____ 8. Pienso mucho en el significado de la vida.

_____ 9. Siempre pienso en el bienestar (*well-being*) de otras personas.

_____ 10. Todos los sábados me paro en una gasolinera para comprar chicle y revistas.

_____ 11. Siempre me empeño en leer un contrato palabra por palabra antes de firmarlo.

_____ 12. Es peligroso montar en un coche con una persona que está borracha (*drunk*).

_____ 13. Las personas obsesionadas con el control siempre insisten en tener la última palabra.

_____ 14. Tengo que confesarlo: Me esfuerzo en aprender cocinar, pero es muy difícil.

_____ 15. Nunca quedo en hacer algo que es peligroso.

Traducción *Translate the following sentences into Spanish, using the preceding list of verbs that require* **en**.

1. *Some people persist in exercising* (hacer ejercicio) *even* (aun) *when they're sick and shouldn't do it.*

   _____

2. *María takes pleasure in playing the guitar at parties.*

   _____

3. *First I think about food, and then I think about eating something in particular.*

   _____

4. *Every day we should reflect on something good in* (de) *this world.*

   _____

5. *At the end* (A finales) *of the month, Marcos always finds himself in a jam* (el apuro).

   _____

6. *When the police arrive, the thief consents to go with them peacefully* (pacíficamente).

   _____

7. *People who gossip* (chismear) *involve themselves in other people's lives.*

   _____

8. *Juan and María agree to consult a psychiatrist* (el psiquiatra).

   _____

9. *Every year I agree to contribute* (donar) *to the Cancer Society.*

   _____

10. *You shouldn't get involved in their problems.*

    _____

11. *I'm not thinking about anything now.*

    _____

12. *My sister never takes the trouble to telephone (me)* (llamar por teléfono).

    _____

13. *I am very interested in international politics* (la política internacional).

    _____

14. *It takes me one hour to drive to the stadium* (el estadio) *from here.*

    _____

15. *For exercise, the children ride bicycles.*

    _____

para

The smallest group of verbs that take a preposition consists of the verbs that take **para**. The preposition **para** often implies moving ahead or toward something. The following verbs indicate that an action is occurring for the purpose of something else to happen—something moves ahead, precipitating something else.

estar listo/lista para (*v.*)	to be ready to (*do something*)
estar para (*v.*)	to be about to (*do something*)
prepararse para (*n./v.*)	to prepare oneself for (*something*), to prepare oneself to (*do something*)
quedarse para (*v.*)	to stay to (*do something*)
sentarse para (*v.*)	to sit down to (*do something*)
servir para (*n./v.*)	to be of use for (*something / doing something*), to serve as (*something*)
trabajar para (*n./v.*)	to work for (*someone [a company]*), to strive to (*do something*)

EJERCICIO

¿Verdadero o falso?

_____ 1. Trabajo para una persona muy simpática y honrada.

_____ 2. Cuando me siento para comer, generalmente tengo conmigo un periódico o una revista.

_____ 3. Para mí, la televisión no sirve para nada.

_____ 4. Estoy listo/lista para tomar el examen final en esta clase de español.

_____ 5. Cada mañana me preparo para el trabajo.

_____ 6. Un diccionario de español sirve para enseñar el idioma y la gramática.

_____ 7. Cuando estoy para dormir, enciendo todas las luces en la casa.

_____ 8. Cada día trabajo para mejorarme y entender más del mundo.

_____ 9. Un buen negociante se queda en la oficina para terminar el trabajo cada noche.

_____ 10. Cuando me preparo para acostarme, siempre me cepillo los dientes.

_____ 11. El anillo de matrimonio sirve para simbolizar el compromiso (*commitment*).

_____ 12. Un contable (*accountant*) trabaja para ahorrar (*to save*) dinero para su cliente.

EJERCICIO
17·7

Traducción *Translate the following sentences into Spanish, using the preceding list of verbs that require* **para**.

1. *Usually it's very late when I sit down to study.*

2. *Martha Stewart says that many things in the garbage can* (la basura) *serve as decorations in the house.*

   _____

3. *Are you ready to leave? Yes, we're ready to leave.*

   _____

4. *We're about to eat lunch* (almorzar).

   _____

5. *I want to work for another company.*

   _____

6. *Do you want to stay to watch the news* (las noticias) *with me?*

   _____

7. *This film is of no use.*

   _____

8. *Every January, many people strive to lose weight* (perder peso).

   _____

9. *Kate needs at least* (por lo menos) *two hours in order to prepare herself for each public appearance* (la aparición pública).

   _____

10. *Mike is preparing himself to find a new job because he works for a real brute* (el bruto).

   _____

por

Verbs that take **por** often deal with emotions (for example, **llorar por**) or convey a feeling of equality in the sense of "on behalf of" (for example, **abogar por**).

The difference between **para** (purpose and destination) and **por** (emotions and equality) is seen in the verb pairs **estar *para*** ("to be about to" do something) and **estar *por*** ("to be in favor of" doing something), as well as **trabajar *para*** ("to work for" someone) and **trabajar *por*** ("to work in place of" or "to work on behalf of" someone).

abogar por (*n.*)	to plead on behalf of (*someone/something*)
acabar por (*v.*)	to end by (*doing something*), to wind up (*doing something*)
apurarse por (*n./v.*)	to worry oneself about (*someone/something / doing something*), to fret over (*someone/something / doing something*)
cambiar por (*n.*)	to exchange (*something*)
clasificar por (*n.*)	to classify in/by (*something*)
dar gracias por (*n./v.*)	to thank for (*something / doing something*), to give thanks for (*something / doing something*)
enviar por (*n.*)	to send via (*something* [*mail, etc.*])
esforzarse por (*n./v.*)	to strive for (*someone/something / doing something*)
estar por (*v.*)	to be inclined to (*do something*), to be in favor of (*doing something*)

hacer por (*v.*)	to try to (*do something*)
impacientarse por (*n./v.*)	to grow impatient for (*someone/something / doing something*), to be impatient to (*do something*)
llorar por (*n./v.*)	to cry for/about (*someone/something / doing something*)
luchar por (*n./v.*)	to struggle for (*someone/something / doing something*)
morirse por (*n./v.*)	to be dying for (*something*), to be dying to (*do something*)
ofenderse por (*n./v.*)	to be offended by (*something / doing something*)
optar por (*n./v.*)	to choose (*something / doing something*), to opt for (*something / doing something*)
preocuparse por (*n./v.*)	to worry about (*someone/something / doing something*)
rabiar por (*n./v.*)	to be crazy about (*someone/something / doing something*)
terminar por (*v.*)	to end by (*doing something*)
trabajar por (*n.*)	to work for (*someone [as a substitute]*)
votar por (*n.*)	to vote for (*someone/something*)

EJERCICIO

¿Verdadero o falso?

_____ 1. Me preocupo mucho por el dinero.

_____ 2. Cuando tengo que decidir entre la televisión o el teatro, usualmente opto por el teatro.

_____ 3. Ben Crump, Mark Geragos y Nancy Grace abogan por sus clientes.

_____ 4. Las personas de Argentina lloran por Evita Perón.

_____ 5. En las elecciones políticas, siempre voto por el candidato más moderado.

_____ 6. Romeo rabia por Julieta.

_____ 7. Puedo comprar más si cambio mis dólares por pesos.

_____ 8. Durante los fines de semana, estoy por dormir mucho y trabajar poco.

_____ 9. A veces doy gracias por las dificultades de la vida.

_____ 10. Cuando un maestro está enfermo, típicamente un sustituto trabaja por él.

_____ 11. Con frecuencia la orquesta termina por tocar algo excepcional.

_____ 12. Si no tengo planes específicos para el fin de semana, usualmente acabo por no hacer nada.

_____ 13. Me esfuerzo por hacer lo mejor que pueda todos los días.

_____ 14. Me impaciento por personas que conducen muy lentamente.

_____ 15. Durante el año, mando muchos regalos por correo.

Traducción *Translate the following sentences into Spanish, using the preceding list of verbs that require* **por.**

1. *Harold worries about losing his teeth and his hair.*

_____

2. *In the novel* Anna Karenina, *Levin struggles always to do the right thing* (lo correcto).

_____

3. *The people* (el pueblo) *of Argentina shouldn't cry for Evita.*

_____

4. *I worry a lot about global warming* (el calentamiento global).

_____

5. *Many people are offended by the waste* (el desperdicio) *of food in restaurants.*

_____

6. *I'm dying to see your new hairdo* (el peinado).

_____

7. *In this office, we classify everything by size* (el tamaño).

_____

8. *Usually a gymnast* (el/la gimnasta) *ends by doing something spectacular* (espectacular).

_____

9. *They always opt for swimming in the river.*

_____

10. *When I have a choice* (la elección) *between two movies, I usually opt for the one that has the better reviews* (la reseña).

_____

11. *Laura is impatient to move* (mudarse) *to another part of the country.*

_____

12. *Many defense lawyers* (el abogado defensor) *plead on behalf of a guilty* (culpable) *person.*

_____

13. *We give you thanks for telling us the truth.*

_____

14. *I always classify my books alphabetically* (orden alfabético).

_____

15. *She always votes for the less attractive candidate.*

_____

Appendix A
The Eight Parts of Speech

1. Noun

A word that represents a person, place, thing, or idea.

jefe	*boss*	casa	*house*
lápiz	*pencil*	libertad	*liberty*

2. Verb

A word that expresses an action, occurrence, or mode of being.

saltar *jump*	llover *rain*	ser *be*

3. Adjective

A word that modifies or describes a noun. It can be descriptive or quantitative.

DESCRIPTIVE

grande *big*	alto *tall*	bello *beautiful*

QUANTITATIVE

varios *several*	muchos *many*	dos *two*

NOTE Articles are classified as definite and indefinite. Technically, articles are adjectives, because they modify nouns; however, many people believe that they deserve separate status due to their frequency of use.

el, la *the*	un, una *a, an*

4. Adverb

A word that modifies or describes a verb, adjective, or other adverb.

allí *there*	muy *very*	lentamente *slowly*

5. Preposition

A word that shows the relationship of a noun or pronoun to another word in a phrase, clause, or sentence.

de *of*	entre *between*	para *for*

6. Interjection

A word or phrase used as an exclamation without any grammatical function.

¡Maravilloso! *Great!*   ¡Caramba! *Darn!*

7. Pronoun

A word that replaces a noun that is understood because of previous use or from context.

él *he*   nuestro *our*   nadie *no one*

8. Conjunction

A word that connects two words, phrases, clauses, or sentences.

y *and*   ni... ni *neither . . . nor*

Appendix B

Pronouns

1. Personal Pronouns

A personal pronoun (also called a subject pronoun) replaces a noun that names the subject or actor in a clause or sentence.

Yo comí un durazno, pero **tú** comiste toda la sandía.

*I ate a peach, but **you** ate all the watermelon.*

SINGULAR		PLURAL	
yo	*I*	nosotros	*we* (masc., masc. & fem.)
		nosotras	*we* (fem.)
tú	*you* (informal)	vosotros	*you* (informal, masc., masc. & fem.)
		vosotras	*you* (informal, fem.)
él	*he*	ellos	*they* (masc., masc. & fem.)
ella	*she*	ellas	*they* (fem.)
usted	*you* (formal)	ustedes	*you* (formal)

2. Interrogative Pronouns

An interrogative pronoun is used in asking questions. The answer sought will be a noun or pronoun (either a person or thing).

¿Quién está en la cárcel?	**Who** *is in jail?*
¿Cuál prefieres?	**Which** *do you prefer?*
¿Quién? ¿Quiénes?	*Who?*
¿A quién? ¿A quiénes?	*(To) Whom?*
¿De quién? ¿De quiénes?	*Whose?*
¿Qué?	*What? Which?*
¿Cuál? ¿Cuáles?	*Which? What?*

3. Prepositional Pronouns

A prepositional pronoun follows a preposition and functions as the object of the preposition, replacing a noun that names a person or thing.

para **mí**	*for **me***
a **usted**	*to **you***
cerca de **ella**	*near **her***

Prepositional pronouns are nearly identical to the subject pronouns, with the exceptions of **mí** and **ti** and the addition of the third-person form **ello**, which represents a masculine or neuter noun.

SINGULAR		PLURAL	
mí	*me*	nosotros	*us* (masc., masc. & fem.)
		nosotras	*us* (fem.)
ti	*you* (informal)	vosotros	*you* (informal, masc., masc. & fem.)
		vosotras	*you* (informal, fem.)
él	*him*	ellos	*them, it* (masc.)
ella	*her, it* (fem.)	ellas	*them, it* (fem.)
usted	*you* (formal)	ustedes	*you* (formal)
ello	*it* (masc., neut.)		

Pronouns with **con**: certain pronouns that follow the preposition **con** ("with") take on a special form.

SINGULAR		PLURAL	
conmigo	*with me*	con nosotros, con nosotras	*with us*
contigo	*with you*	con vosotros, con vosotras	*with you*
consigo	*with him, with her, with you*	consigo	*with them, with you*

In certain situations, the standard prepositional pronouns are used with **con** ("with") in the third person, as shown below.

SINGULAR		PLURAL	
con él	*with him*	con ellos	*with them*
con ella	*with her, it*	con ellas	*with them*
con usted	*with you*	con ustedes	*with you*
con ello	*with it*		

Subject pronouns with prepositions: in Spanish, there are six prepositions that always take a subject pronoun, rather than a standard prepositional pronoun.

entre	*between*	menos	*except*
excepto	*except*	salvo	*except*
incluso	*including*	según	*according to*

Reflexive pronouns following a preposition: a reflexive action (an action that "reflects" back on the performer) can be expressed with a preposition followed by a reflexive pronoun.

a mí mismo	*to myself*	a nosotros mismos	*to ourselves*
a mí misma	*to myself*	a nosotras mismas	*to ourselves*
a ti mismo	*to yourself*	a vosotros mismos	*to yourselves*
a ti misma	*to yourself*	a vosotras mismas	*to yourselves*
a sí mismo	*to himself, to yourself, to itself*	a sí mismos	*to themselves, yourselves*
a sí misma	*to herself, to yourself, to itself*	a sí mismas	*to themselves, yourselves*

4. Possessive Pronouns

A possessive pronoun replaces the nouns that name the owner of an object and the object itself.

| El sapo es **mío**. | *The toad is **mine**.* |
| Una amiga **tuya** canta muy bien. | *A friend **of yours** sings very well.* |

SINGULAR		PLURAL	
mío, míos	*mine*	nuestro, nuestros	*ours*
mía, mías	*mine*	nuestra, nuestras	*ours*
tuyo, tuyos	*yours*	vuestro, vuestros	*yours*
tuya, tuyas	*yours*	vuestra, vuestras	*yours*
suyo, suyos	*his, hers, yours, its*	suyo, suyos	*theirs, yours*
suya, suyas	*his, hers, yours, its*	suya, suyas	*theirs, yours*

5. Demonstrative Pronouns

A demonstrative pronoun replaces an understood noun and points out its location relative to the speaker.

| Me gustan las dos camisas, pero prefiero **ésa**. | *I like both shirts, but I prefer **that one**.* |

	MASCULINE	FEMININE	NEUTER
this (one)	éste	ésta	esto
these (ones)	éstos	éstas	
that (one)	ése	ésa	eso
those (ones)	ésos	ésas	
that over there	aquél	aquélla	aquello
those over there	aquéllos	aquéllas	

6. Numbers as Pronouns

A number used as a pronoun replaces an understood or omitted noun. It assumes the meaning of the noun itself as well as the number.

| Las tortitas son deliciosas. Dame **una**, por favor. | *The cupcakes are delicious. Give me **one**, please.* |
| De todos los coches que probamos, me gusta más el **segundo**. | *Of all the cars we tried out, I like the **second one** best.* |

CARDINAL NUMBERS (one, two, three, . . .)	ORDINAL NUMBERS (first, second, third, . . .)
uno, una	primero, primera
dos	segundo, segunda
tres	tercero, tercera
cuatro	cuarto, cuarta
cinco	quinto, quinta
seis	sexto, sexta
siete	séptimo, séptima
ocho	octavo, octava
nueve	noveno, novena
diez	décimo, décima

7. Adjective Pronouns

An adjective pronoun is an adjective that assumes the meaning of an understood, irrelevant, or omitted noun. Descriptive, or qualitative, adjectives easily become pronouns.

¡Anoche Carmen salió con un **anciano**! [hombre *is understood*]	*Last night Carmen went out with an **old man**!*
Tú compraste los platos azules, pero yo compré los **blancos**. [platos *is omitted, previously stated*]	*You bought the blue plates, but I bought the **white (ones)**.*

Many adjective pronouns are quantitative pronouns that correspond to indefinite pronouns in English. Others are adjectives with "clipped"—or omitted—words, which many times refer to unspecified people or things.

Nadie vino a la fiesta.	***No one** came to the party.*
Te di tu invitación, pero mandé **las demás** por correo.	*I gave you your invitation, but I sent **the rest** by mail.*

Below are several frequently used adjective pronouns; some are quantitative and others refer to unspecified nouns.

algo	*something, anything*
alguien	*somebody, someone*
algunos, algunas	*some (of them), any (of them)*
ambos, ambas	*both*
cada	*each*
cada uno, cada una	*each one*
cualquiera	*anyone, anybody, any one (person), anything, whichever, whatever*
cualesquiera	*any people [pl.], any [pl.]*
demasiado, demasiada	*too much*
demasiados, demasiadas	*too many*
el/la mayor	*the oldest (one)*
el/la menor	*the youngest (one)*
lo mejor	*the best (thing)*
lo mismo	*the same (thing)*
lo peor	*the worst (thing)*
los dos, las dos	*both*
los otros, las otras	*the others*
mucho, mucha	*much, a lot of*
muchos, muchas	*many, a lot of*
nada	*nothing*
nadie	*nobody, no one*
ninguno, ninguna	*none, not anything, neither one*
otro, otra	*another, the other*
poco, poca	*(a) little*
pocos, pocas	*few*
todo	*everything, all*
todos, todas	*everyone, everybody*
último, última	*last*
unos, unas	*some*
unos cuantos, unas cuantas	*a few (of them)*
varios, varias	*several*

8. Relative Pronouns

A relative pronoun represents understood or omitted material and connects a dependent clause with an independent, or principal, clause.

Las personas **que** viven allí son muy simpáticas.	*The people **who** live there are very nice.*
Ella es la señora con **quien** trabajo.	*She is the lady with **whom** I work.*
Lo **que** debes hacer es ganar la lotería.	***What** you should do is win the lottery.*

Below are several frequently used relative pronouns.

cuyo, cuya, cuyos, cuyas	*whose*
el cual, la cual	*the one who, the one that*
el que, la que	*the one who, the one that*
lo que	*that which, what, whatever*
los cuales, las cuales	*those who, those that*
los que, las que	*those who, those that*
que	*that, who, which, that which* (following a preposition)
quien, quienes	*whom* (following a preposition)

9. Direct Object Pronouns

A direct object pronoun replaces a noun that names the direct object of the verb in a sentence or clause. It answers the question "What?" or "Whom?"

¿Ese libro? **Lo** leí. ¿Cuándo vas a leer**lo** tú?	*That book? I read **it**. When are you going to read **it**?*
Tú ya no **me** amas, pero yo sigo queriéndo**te**.	*You don't love **me** anymore, but I still love **you**.*

SINGULAR		PLURAL	
me	*me*	nos	*us*
te	*you*	os	*you*
lo	*him, you, it*	los	*them, you*
la	*her, you, it*	las	*them, you*

10. Indirect Object Pronouns

An indirect object pronoun replaces a noun that names the indirect object of the verb in a sentence or clause. It answers the questions "To whom?" and "For whom?"

Juan siempre **le** da una rosa blanca a María.	*Juan always gives **María** a white rose.*
¡No **me** digas mentiras!	*Don't tell **me** lies!*
No he oído el último chiste. Cuénta**me**lo, por favor.	*I haven't heard the latest joke. Tell it to **me**, please.*

SINGULAR		PLURAL	
me	*me*	nos	*us*
te	*you*	os	*you*
le	*him, her, it, you*	les	*them, you*

11. Reflexive Object Pronouns

A reflexive object pronoun indicates that the subject and the object of an action are the same person or thing.

Me veo en el espejo.	*I see myself in the mirror.*
Nos cepillamos los dientes tres veces al día.	*We brush our teeth three times a day.*

SINGULAR		PLURAL	
me	*myself*	nos	*ourselves*
te	*yourself*	os	*yourselves*
se	*himself, herself, itself, yourself*	se	*themselves, yourselves*

12. Double-Object Pronoun Order: RID

RID is an acronym that is useful for remembering the placement order for two object pronouns in a sentence. Two object pronouns in a sentence are always used in the following order: *reflexive* object pronoun, *indirect* object pronoun, *direct* object pronoun.

Me encanta tu pelo. ¿**Te** [R] **lo** [D] lavas mucho?	*I love your hair. Do you wash **it** a lot?*
Él no sabe la verdad. **Se** [I] **la** [D] debemos decir.	*He doesn't know the truth. We should tell **it to him**.*

In the second example, the indirect and direct object pronouns could also be attached to the infinitive: **Debemos decírsela**. Note that an accent mark is usually required to retain the original stress in the infinitive. Also note that whenever the two object pronouns begin with the letter *l*, the *l* in the first pronoun changes to *s*: **Le la debemos decir** becomes **Se la debemos decir**.

Following are patterns for the more common combinations of double object pronouns.

R + D + CONJUGATED VERB	I + D + CONJUGATED VERB
OR	OR
INFINITIVE + R + D	INFINITIVE + I + D

13. Reciprocal Pronouns

A reciprocal pronoun expresses reciprocity; it indicates an action that goes back and forth between two or more subjects.

Nos conocimos ayer.	*We met each other yesterday.*
Se hablan mucho.	*They talk to one another a lot.*

nos	*each other, each of us, one another*
os	*each other, each of you, one another*
se	*each other, each of them, each of you, one another*

14. The Pronoun **Se** and the Passive Voice

Se is commonly used to indicate that an action is performed by an unspecified subject, expressing the passive voice in Spanish.

La cena **se comió** junto al lago.	*Dinner **was eaten** by the lake.*

Se also is used to express an unknown, impersonal subject.

En este colegio **se estudia** mucho.	*In this high school, **one studies** a lot.* *In this high school, **they study** a lot.*
¡No **se debe** fumar nunca!	***One should** never smoke!* ***You should** never smoke!*

Actions involving inanimate objects often employ **se**.

Mi coche **se** me **descompone** todo el tiempo.	*My car **breaks down** on me all the time.*
Los cristales **se quebraron** cuando ella cantó.	*The glassware **broke** when she sang.*

The pattern using **se** to express the passive voice is shown below.

se + THIRD-PERSON CONJUGATED VERB

Appendix C

Prepositions

Prepositions that show a relationship between nouns and/or pronouns

acerca de	*about*
además de	*besides, in addition to*
con	*with*
contra	*against*
en lugar de	*instead of*
en vez de	*instead of*
excepto	*except*
menos	*except*
salvo	*except*
según	*according to*
sin	*without*
sobre	*about, on* (topic)

Prepositions of location

a	*at*
a la derecha de	*to the right of*
a la izquierda de	*to the left of*
a través de	*across*
al lado de	*next to, next door to*
cerca de	*near, close to*
con	*with*
debajo de	*under*
delante de	*in front of*
dentro de	*inside*
detrás de	*behind*
en	*in, at, on*
encima de	*on top of*
enfrente de	*across from, opposite*
entre (*dos personas o cosas*)	*between* (two people or things)
entre (*varias personas o cosas*)	*among* (several people or things)
frente a	*facing*
fuera de	*outside*
junto a	*by, next to, next door to*
lejos de	*far from*
sobre	*on top of, above*

Prepositions of movement

a lo largo de	*along*
alrededor de	*around*
hacia	*toward*
más allá de	*beyond*
por	*through, throughout*

Prepositions of geographical orientation

al este de	*(to the) east of*
al nordeste/noreste de	*(to the) northeast of*
al noroeste de	*(to the) northwest of*
al norte de	*(to the) north of*
al oeste de	*(to the) west of*
al sudeste/sureste de	*(to the) southeast of*
al sudoeste/suroeste de	*(to the) southwest of*
al sur de	*(to the) south of*

Prepositions of origin and destination

Origin

a causa de	*because of, for*
de	*from, of*
de (*to indicate authorship*)	*by*
desde	*(all the way) from*
por	*because of, for*
por (*to indicate authorship*)	*by*

Destination

a	*to*
hacia	*toward*
para (*purpose/destination*)	*for*

Prepositions of time

a	*to, until*
antes de	*before*
desde	*since*
después de	*after*
durante	*during*
hasta	*until*
por	*through*

The uses of **para** and **por**

Para

1. Destination
   a. To indicate real or imagined destination
   b. To express the recipient of an action
   c. To indicate direction and/or final destination
   d. To indicate an action's aim or objective, including profession

2. Purpose
    a. To express purpose before an infinitive
    b. To indicate purpose for doing something; "in order to" before an infinitive
3. Deadline
    a. To express a specific time limit or deadline in the future
    b. To express a limited time span in the future
4. Standard
    a. To express a comparison to a certain standard
    b. To express an opinion or personal standard

Por

1. Duration
    a. To express duration of time
    b. To indicate periods of time during the 24-hour day
    c. To express English use of Latin *per*
2. Substitution or exchange
    a. To indicate an equal exchange or trade
    b. To express substitution ("on behalf of," "in place of")
    c. To express thanks and gratitude
3. Motivation
    a. To indicate "because of" or having done something (**por** + INFINITIVE)
    b. To express a motive for doing something
    c. To express a reason for something (**por** + NOUN or **por** + INFINITIVE)
4. Movement
    a. To express means of transportation
    b. To express means of sending messages or information
    c. To indicate the point of an intermediate destination
    d. To indicate movement in an area
5. Emotions
    a. To express a like (or dislike) or an emotion for someone or something
6. Idioms
    a. To appear in idiomatic expressions

Answer Key

 **PRONOUNS**

1 Subject Pronouns

1·1
1. yo
2. nosotros/nosotras
3. ellos/ellas/ustedes
4. él/ella/usted
5. vosotros/vosotras
6. nosotros/nosotras
7. él/ella/usted
8. ellos/ellas/ustedes
9. vosotros/vosotras
10. tú

11. él/ella/usted
12. yo
13. tú
14. vosotros/vosotras
15. él/ella/usted
16. yo
17. tú
18. nosotros/nosotras
19. ellos/ellas/ustedes
20. tú

1·2
1. yo tengo
2. tú tienes
3. él quiere
4. nosotros estamos
5. vosotros salís
6. ellos/ellas/ustedes quieren
7. yo puedo
8. ella viene
9. nosotros/nosotras somos
10. tú sales

11. usted juega
12. yo pongo
13. ustedes ponen
14. ellos dicen
15. vosotros/vosotras estáis
16. tú oyes
17. ellas pueden
18. nosotros vemos
19. nosotros/nosotras oímos
20. vosotros/vosotras veis

1·3
1. Yo
2. ella
3. Nosotros
4. Ellas

5. tú
6. vosotros
7. usted
8. Ellos

2 Interrogative Pronouns

2·1
1. ¿Quién es ella?
2. ¿Quiénes son ellos?
3. ¿Quién eres? OR ¿Quién es usted?
4. ¿Quién soy yo?
5. ¿Quién trabaja aquí?
6. ¿Quién mira la televisión?
7. ¿Quién habla español aquí?
8. ¿Quién no vive aquí?
9. ¿Quién escribe el libro?
10. ¿Quién es tu (OR su) amigo?

2·2
1. ¿A quién amas?
2. ¿A quién ves?
3. ¿A quién miras?
4. ¿A quiénes miras?
5. ¿A quién buscas?
6. ¿A quiénes buscas?
7. ¿A quién escuchas?
8. ¿A quiénes escuchas?
9. ¿A quién conoces?
10. ¿A quiénes conoces?

2·3
1. ¿De quién es este coche?
2. ¿De quién son las llaves que están en la mesa?
3. ¿De quiénes son los coches que están sucios?
4. ¿De quiénes son las niñas que leen estos libros?
5. ¿De quién es el gato que bebe la leche?
6. ¿De quién son los vecinos que viven en la casa azul?
7. ¿De quiénes son los estudiantes más inteligentes?
8. ¿De quién es el coche que no funciona?
9. ¿De quién es este abrigo?
10. ¿De quién es el loro que habla italiano?
11. ¿De quiénes son estos discos compactos?
12. ¿De quién es esta mochila?

2·4
1. ¿Qué libro es más interesante?
2. ¿Qué actor es más popular?
3. ¿Qué chica es tu prima?
4. ¿Qué comida tiene más grasa?
5. ¿Qué tienda vende más ropa?
6. ¿Cuál comes más, el pollo o el pescado?
7. ¿Cuál es más popular?
8. ¿Cuáles llevas más?
9. ¿Qué zapatos llevas más?
10. ¿Qué sombrero es más cómodo?
11. ¿Cuál de los sombreros es más cómodo?
12. ¿Qué programa miras?
13. ¿Cuáles de los nuevos programas miras?
14. ¿Cuáles miras?

2·5
1. ¿Qué?, ¿Qué día es hoy?
2. ¿Cuál?, ¿Cuál es la fecha de hoy?
3. ¿Cuál?,¿Cuál es su nombre?
4. ¿Qué?, ¿Qué hora es?
5. ¿Cuál?, ¿Cuál es tu razón por esto?

6. ¿Qué?, ¿Qué es eso?
7. ¿Qué?, ¿Qué libro quieres tú?
8. ¿Cuál?, ¿Cuáles quieres?
9. ¿Qué?, ¿Qué mujer es tu amiga?
10. ¿Qué?, ¿Qué significa esto?
11. ¿Cuál?, ¿Cuál es la respuesta?
12. ¿Qué?, ¿Qué quieres saber?
13. ¿Cuál?, ¿Cuál es tu nombre?
14. ¿Cuál?, ¿Cuál es tu dirección?

3   Prepositional Pronouns

3·1
1. Él tiene un libro para mí.
2. Tengo un regalo para ti.
3. ¿Qué tienes para mí?
4. La mesa es de ella.
5. Compro mis libros de ellos.
6. Ella corre delante de nosotros.
7. Estás detrás de él.
8. Él vive cerca de mí.
9. La alfombra está debajo de nosotras.
10. Él vive cerca de ustedes (OR vosotros OR vosotras).
11. Él escribe un libro acerca de ella.
12. Caminamos detrás de ellos.
13. Ella baila a la derecha de mí.
14. Ellos trabajan a la izquierda de ti.
15. La comida está delante de nosotros.

3·2
1. Estoy contigo.
2. Usted está conmigo.
3. Ella está con él.
4. Él está con ella.
5. Trabajo contigo ahora.
6. Ellos viven conmigo.
7. ¿Estudia ella contigo?
8. ¿Quién vive con ustedes?
9. ¿Por qué no quieres trabajar con él?
10. Quiero hablar con usted.
11. Él vive con nosotros.
12. Ella siempre lleva las llaves consigo.
13. Ellos nunca llevan las llaves consigo.
14. La fuerza está contigo.
15. ¿Por qué no lleva (usted) el paraguas consigo?
16. ¿Por qué no llevan (ellas) el paraguas consigo?

3·3
1. Hay veinte personas aquí, incluso tú y yo.
2. Según ella, el dinero puede comprar la felicidad.
3. Entre tú, yo y el piano de cola, esta pintura es espantosa.
4. Creo que todo el mundo aquí habla alemán, menos (OR excepto OR salvo) yo.
5. Entre nosotros y ellos, tenemos suficiente dinero.
6. Todos aquí están escandalizados, incluso yo.
7. Todos en la vecindad tienen una piscina salvo (OR menos OR excepto) nosotros.
8. Tenemos muchas dificultades, según yo.
9. Todos están listos, excepto (OR menos OR salvo) usted.
10. Según ellos, es posible vivir en Marte.

3·4
1. Compro el coche para mí mismo.
2. Él hace todo para sí mismo.
3. Ellos hacen todo por sí mismos.
4. Ella perjudica a sí misma cuando dice una mentira.
5. Sólo perjudicáis a vosotras mismas.
6. Escribo notas a mí misma para recordar las cosas que necesito hacer.
7. Debes tener tiempo para ti mismo cada día.
8. Ella siempre compra un regalo para sí misma en su cumpleaños.
9. Cuando viajo, envío (OR mando) mis compras a mí misma por correo.
10. Usted no puede vender su casa a sí mismo. ¡Es ridículo!

3·5
Pedro es mi amigo. Estoy muy feliz porque vive al lado de mí. Un mapache vive debajo de mi casa. Entre ustedes (OR vosotros) y yo, creo que los mapaches son animales interesantes. Leo (OR Estoy leyendo) un libro acerca de ellos ahora. Usualmente el mapache vive en un árbol, pero tengo suerte porque mi casa está encima de este mapache. Según Pedro, el mapache es parte de la familia del oso, y él cree que si ve el animal delante de él, es "adiós, mundo." Cuando Pedro sale de o entra en mi casa, siempre mira a la izquierda y después a la derecha.

4   Possessive Pronouns

4·1
1. Es mío.
2. Es tuya.
3. Es suyo.
4. Son mías.
5. Son suyos.
6. Es nuestra.
7. Son tuyas.
8. Son vuestros.
9. Son suyas.
10. Es vuestra.
11. Son mías.
12. Son tuyas.
13. Son nuestras.
14. Es suya.
15. Es suyo.

4·2
1. El gato es mío. Las gatas son mías.
2. La culebra es tuya (OR vuestra OR suya). Las culebras son tuyas (OR vuestras OR suyas).
3. El pájaro es suyo. Los pájaros son suyos.
4. El mono es suyo. Los monos son suyos.
5. La jirafa es nuestra. Las jirafas son nuestras.
6. El cerdo es suyo. Los cerdos son suyos.
7. La araña es mía. Las arañas son mías.
8. El caballo es tuyo (OR vuestro OR suyo). Los caballos son tuyos (OR vuestros OR suyos).
9. La mariposa es suya. Las mariposas son suyas.
10. El elefante es nuestro. Los elefantes son nuestros.

4·3
1. Un amigo mío trabaja aquí.
2. Una amiga mía vive aquí.
3. Algunos (OR Unos) amigos míos tienen una cabaña en Canadá.
4. Una amiga suya estudia español.
5. Trabajo con una amiga tuya.
6. Un colega nuestro habla alemán y gaélico.
7. Ellos no quieren hablar con él porque es un enemigo suyo.
8. Un amigo tuyo es un amigo mío.
9. Esas pinturas suyas son fascinantes.
10. Una prima nuestra es una princesa en Europa.

4·4
1. Su casa está sucia, pero la nuestra está limpia.
2. Sus libros están en la cocina y los míos están en el comedor.
3. Él guarda su dinero en el banco, pero (yo) guardo el mío debajo del colchón.
4. Sus primos viven en Hollywood y los suyos viven en Seattle.
5. Nuestro perro es un perro pastor, y el suyo es un perro de lana.
6. Sus joyas son imitaciones, pero las mías son auténticas.
7. Ellos compran la comida en el supermercado, pero (nosotros) cultivamos la nuestra.
8. Su abogado trabaja para una firma grande. El nuestro tiene una oficina en un sótano.
9. Es mi vida. No es la tuya.
10. Vosotros tenéis vuestros problemas y yo tengo los míos.

4·5
1. Su casa es más grande que la mía.
2. Mi casa no es tan grande como la suya.
3. Su ropa es más cara (OR costosa) que la mía.
4. Vuestras joyas son más elegantes que las nuestras.
5. Su hurón no es tan amable como el nuestro.
6. Su termo no está tan lleno como el mío.
7. El reportaje de María es más interesante que el suyo.
8. El portatíl de Juan es más nuevo que el suyo.
9. Sus sobres son más bonitos que los míos. Voy a comprar una caja.
10. Sus martillos no son tan pesados como los tuyos.

4·6
1. Tu coche es mejor que el mío.
2. Sus sillas son mejores que las nuestras.
3. Mi pintura es peor que la suya.
4. Las cortinas de Elena son peores que las suyas.
5. Su amigo es mayor que el mío.
6. Mis abuelos son mayores que los tuyos.
7. Nuestro hijo es menor que el vuestro.
8. Nuestras carpas doradas son menores que las suyas.
9. La paella de Julia es mejor que la mía.
10. La música de Beethoven es mejor que la suya.

4·7
Estoy muy disgustado/disgustada porque Silvia tiene mi anillo. Ella dice que es suyo, pero yo sé que es mío porque tiene mis iniciales. Silvia es cleptómana. Nada en su casa es suya. Muchas cosas son mías. Por ejemplo, todas las pinturas son mías, el reloj de péndulo es mío, el candelabro en el comedor es mío, la lavadora y la secadora son mías, hasta la comida en el refrigerador es mía. ¿Qué puedo hacer? El famoso abogado Perry Mason (de la televisión clásica) dice que la posesión es el noventa y nueve por ciento de la ley. Por eso, todo es suyo. ¡Figurate!

5 Demonstrative Pronouns

5·1
1. Este libro es mío, pero ése es suyo.
2. Esta casa es bonita, pero ésa es más bonita.
3. Estos zapatos son míos y ésos son suyos.
4. Estas sillas son suyas y ésas son mías.
5. Aquel chico es mi vecino y éste es mi hijo.
6. Estas mujeres son mis vecinas, pero aquéllas son de otra ciudad.
7. Ese portatíl es de Juan y aquél es mío.
8. Esas revistas son terribles, pero éstas son mucho mejores.
9. Este teléfono celular funciona, pero aquél nunca funciona.
10. Estos programas son terribles, pero ésos son aún peores.

5.2   1. ¡Esto es fantástico!
      2. ¿Qué es esto?
      3. Eso es un crimen.
      4. Yo nunca hago eso.
      5. Esto es un pecado.
      6. ¿Qué pasa con aquello?
      7. Eso es por qué debes votar.
      8. Esto es por qué no debo fumar.
      9. ¿Quién dice eso?
     10. ¿Quién escribe esto?
     11. ¿Quién tiene eso?
     12. ¿Por qué hagan esto?

5.3   "¿Quién necesita esto? ¡Esto es tan estúpido! No necesito esto para mi trabajo." Algunas personas dicen esto cuando están frustradas o cuando tienen que tomar una clase en la universidad que no quieren tomar. Es esta clase o ésa. Es este profesor o ése. Son estos libros o ésos. Son estas tareas o ésas. ¿Cuándo termina esto? ¿Termina esto después de la graduación? Quizás. Espero que sí. La vida es lo que tú haces de ella.

6   Numbers as Pronouns

6.1   1. ¿Cuántos coches tienes? Tengo uno.
      2. ¿Cuántas casas tienes? Tengo una.
      3. ¿Cuántas galletas quieres? Quiero diez.
      4. ¿Cuántas hamburguesas quieren? Jane quiere dos y yo quiero una.
      5. ¿Cuántas personas hay en tu familia? Hay tres.
      6. Él tiene siete perros, pero yo sólo tengo seis.
      7. Él ve muchas estrellas en el cielo, pero yo veo sólo una.
      8. María conoce todas estas pinturas, pero nosotros conocemos sólo una.
      9. Tengo sólo una silla, pero una es mejor que nada.
     10. ¿Cuántos naipes quieres? Quiero uno.

6.2   1. el séptimo   6. el primero
      2. la segunda   7. la octava
      3. el noveno   8. el tercero
      4. el quinto   9. el sexto
      5. la décima   10. la cuarta

6.3   1. Yo vivo en la segunda casa a la izquierda y Miguel vive en la sexta.
      2. ¿Quién vive en la octava casa? No sé, pero Marcos vive en la séptima.
      3. Mi coche es el tercero a la derecha, y el coche de Ricardo es el cuarto.
      4. La Biblia dice que Adán es la primera persona y que Eva es la segunda.
      5. La primera película usualmente es mejor que la segunda.
      6. La tercera película del actor es mejor que la cuarta.
      7. Su quinto libro es más interesante que el sexto.
      8. En España, el primer día de la semana es lunes y el séptimo es domingo.
      9. El octavo mes es agosto, el noveno es septiembre y el décimo es octubre.
     10. El primer rompecabezas es más difícil que el segundo.
     11. Hoy es el primero del otoño.
     12. La primera vez siempre es mejor que la segunda, la tercera y así sucesivamente.

6.4   Cuando comemos juntos, mi amigo y yo competimos para ver quién puede comer más. Por ejemplo, cuando comemos galletas, si yo como una, él come dos. Entonces yo como tres y él come cuatro. El primer participante con un plato vacío es el ganador. Esto es fácil con galletas o uvas o cerezas. Pero es muy difícil con hamburguesas. La primera está sabrosa. La segunda, también. La tercera no está mal. La cuarta es un reto. La quinta es absurda—también la sexta, la séptima y la octava. La novena es pura tortura. Y la décima es imposible. ¡Es peor con los pasteles!

7 Adjective Pronouns

7·1
1. Él compra coches nuevos, pero yo siempre compro los usados.
2. Ella prefiere los hombres altos, pero yo prefiero los bajos.
3. Ellos quieren la pregunta fácil, pero nosotros queremos la difícil.
4. Ella cree que el hombre rubio es guapo, pero yo prefiero el moreno.
5. La pluma azul es tuya, pero la verde es mía.
6. Casi cada cliente quiere comprar un coche de lujo, pero compra el compacto.
7. Más personas compran la alfombra gris porque la blanca siempre está sucia.
8. Los dos vestidos cortos son hermosos, pero el largo es más elegante.
9. Él pone las lámparas grandes en la sala y las pequeñas en el dormitorio.
10. La copa grande es para el vino rojo y la pequeña es para el blanco.

7·2
1. Algunas personas viven en la ciudad y algunas viven en el campo.
2. El setenta por ciento de los dentistas usan este cepillo de dientes y los demás usan un palo.
3. No puedo decidir cuál es el mejor lavaplatos. Me gustan los dos (OR ambos).
4. Nunca voy de compras con ella. Compra todo. Es peligroso.
5. A Diego le gustan las fiestas. Siempre es el último en salir.
6. Mi gato bebe (OR toma) leche todo el tiempo. Por eso, compro mucha cada semana.
7. Tengo varios libros de español. ¿Quieres uno?
8. A Esmeralda le encantan los zapatos. Tiene muchos.
9. En las reuniones, unas cuantas personas hablan todo el tiempo y la mayoría sufre en silencio.
10. Marcia recibe todos los regalos y pobrecita Jan no recibe ninguno.
11. Tenemos mucha ensalada. ¿Quieres más?
12. Usualmente, miles de personas vienen a la ceremonia, pero este año obviamente hay menos.
13. Los estudiantes van de excursión. Cada uno tiene una mochila.
14. Cada chica tiene un lápiz, pero varias no tienen papel.
15. Voy a pedir otro batido. ¿Quieres otro también?

7·3
1. A menudo el menor lleva la ropa usada.
2. Todos creen que esto es brillante.
3. Nadie va a comer esto. ¡Está mohoso!
4. Alguien está en la cocina con Dinah.
5. Nuestra cliente favorita, la que gasta mucho de su dinero en los cosméticos y la ropa, está aquí hoy.
6. En los libros de Harry Potter, Hermione es la mayor y Harry es el menor de los tres personajes principales.
7. Los que trabajan diez horas al día en estos puestos están bien remunerados.
8. Muchos psicólogos estudian las diferencias entre el mayor y el menor en la familia.
9. Oscar Wilde escribe que un cínico es el que sabe el precio de todo y el valor de nada.
10. Todos sufren de vez en cuando, y la mayoría son más fuertes por la experiencia.
11. Todos están aquí, pero algunos no conocen a nadie.
12. Juan y Mateo viven juntos, pero ninguno tiene un televisor.
13. Cualquiera puede llevar estos pantalones.
14. Ramón da consejos a cualquiera.
15. Hay una fiesta esta noche. Cualesquiera de ustedes (OR vosotros) pueden ir conmigo.

7·4

1. ¿Tienes algo para mí?
2. De todas las cosas en el mundo, lo mejor es el amor.
3. No importa si yo llevo blue-jeans. Ella siempre lleva lo mismo.
4. ¿Cuál quieren ellos? Cualquiera. No importa.
5. Es maravilloso cuando ustedes bailan. Lo mejor es cuando bailan el mambo.
6. El servicio y el ambiente aquí son terribles. Pero lo peor es la comida.
7. Él nunca trae nada a una fiesta, pero siempre come y bebe todo.
8. Lo peor en una relación es no poder tener confianza en la otra persona.
9. Algunas personas creen que él es muy sabio, pero la verdad es que siempre dice lo mismo.
10. No sé nada acerca de esto.
11. Cualquiera de estos coches es bueno para el invierno.
12. Estos libros son interesantes. Puedes leer cualquiera de ellos.
13. Cualquiera de estos tres está bien.
14. Cualesquiera de estos están bien.

7·5   Este letrero dice: "Hoy es el primer día del resto de la vida". Si esto es verdad, entonces, ¿qué es mañana? ¿El segundo? No puedo creer todo lo que leo. Nadie puede. Algunos creen todo. Algunas personas creen los anuncios en las contraportadas de las revistas. Supongo que algunos de estos son la verdad, pero la mayoría de estos anuncios son mentiras. ¿Quiénes son estos buhoneros? Prometen todo y no entregan nada.

8   Relative Pronouns

8·1

1. Tengo el libro que quieres. Tenemos las cosas que necesitas.
2. Las personas que trabajan aquí son muy amables.
3. El coche que quiero es rojo.
4. Sólo miro películas que son de España.
5. Él cree que esta salsa está muy picante.
6. La medicina que tomo cada mañana sabe a gasolina.
7. Tienes dos libros que son buenos y dos que son malos.
8. La pintura que ves es por (OR de) Francisco Goya.
9. Él no sabe que yo tengo su cartera.
10. ¿Sabes que la mantequilla es pura grasa?
11. El hombre que vive en esta casa es un plomero.
12. Ellos no saben lo que dicen.
13. Ella es la vieja que vive en un zapato.
14. Los gatos que tienen muchos dedos viven en Key West, Florida.
15. Las personas que votan creen que tienen mucho poder.

8·2

1. Su esposa, la cual (OR la que) es linda, habla cuatro idiomas.
2. Su perro, el cual (OR el que) es un perro de lana, ladra todo el tiempo.
3. Nuestra casa, la cual (OR la que) tiene cien años, es conocida por los fantasmas que viven en el desván.
4. Mis anillos, los cuales (OR los que) son de plata, son de Taxco, México.
5. Nuestros libros, los cuales (OR los que) todavía están en cajas, son muy valiosos.
6. El casero, el cual (OR el que) también vive en este edificio, es un hombre muy extraño.
7. Los niños (OR hijos) de mi vecino, los cuales (OR los que) son más ruidosos que un aeropuerto, están angelitos en la iglesia.
8. La poeta, la cual (OR la que) es la madre de dos hijas, escribe todos los días a la medianoche.
9. La Casa Blanca, la cual (OR la que) es popular con los turistas, es el hogar del presidente de los Estados Unidos.
10. Estos vinos, los cuales (OR los que) son de Francia, tienen noventa años.
11. Este párrafo, el cual (OR el que) acabo de leer, no tiene sentido.
12. Esta actitud de indiferencia, la cual (OR la que) no puedo tolerar, es contagiosa.

8·3
1. Kitty es la mujer con quien vivo.
2. ¿Quién es el hombre con quien vives?
3. Éstas son las personas para quienes él trabaja.
4. El hombre a la izquierda es la persona con quien salgo.
5. Margo es la mujer para quien trabajo.
6. Francisco es el hombre en quien pienso.
7. Kim es la mujer con quien Roberto y Jesse están enojados.
8. Bárbara es la persona por quien tengo compasión.
9. Ana es la mujer a quien veo.
10. Esos hombres son los jugadores a quienes miro.

8·4
1. Él nunca recuerda lo que (yo) quiero.
2. Ella siempre come lo que (yo) como.
3. En tu cumpleaños, puedes pedir lo que quieras.
4. Lo que él dice siempre es mentira.
5. ¿Oyes (tú) lo que (yo) oigo? ¿Sabes (tú) lo que (yo) sé?
6. No comprende lo que lee.
7. Algunas personas siempre hacen lo que no deben hacer. Ellos son sociópatas.
8. ¿Sabes lo que quieres hacer este fin de semana?
9. Ella come exactamente lo que es malo para ella, y por eso siempre está enferma.
10. Lo que (tú) necesitas es un abrazo.

8·5
1. Marcos, cuya madre es dentista, quiere vender dulces.
2. El chico, cuyo libro tienes, es mi primo.
3. El actor, cuyas películas son terribles, es muy rico.
4. El dentista, cuyo consultorio está en la ciudad, vive en las afueras.
5. Los niños, cuyos padres hablan sólo inglés, estudian español.
6. Él es el hombre cuyo perro siempre roba nuestro periódico.
7. ¿Es usted la mujer cuyo árbol es tan hermoso?
8. ¿Son ellos los niños cuyo padre es el senador de Colorado?
9. El estudiante, cuya maestra es de Ecuador, quiere ir a Quito este verano.
10. La vieja señora Hubbard, cuyos gabinetes están vacíos, quiere dar a su perro un hueso.
11. Mark, cuyo padre es presidente de un banco, no puede sumar.
12. Lilia, cuya tienda es muy popular, es mi mejor amiga.

8·6
1. que
2. lo que
3. que
4. cuyo
5. a quien
6. con quienes
7. cuya
8. Lo que
9. que
10. lo que
11. lo que
12. que
13. a quien
14. lo que
15. cuyo

8·7
Cabo San Lucas, que (OR el cual OR el que) está en la punta sureña de Baja California, es un lugar maravilloso para vacaciones tranquilas. El área, que (OR la cual OR la que) es principalmente en el desierto, tiene muchos resortes elegantes que (OR los cuales OR los que) tienen piscinas, restaurantes, bares, tiendas y clubes. En su mayor parte, usted puede hacer lo que quiera en la soledad de su habitación. Hay un centro, el cual (OR que OR el que) es algo pequeño, que tiene una marina, la que (OR que OR la cual) tiene muchos barcos para la pesca. Los turistas que quieren ir de pesca pueden alquilar un barco con un guía. Cualquier persona cuya idea de diversión es (el) calor y (el) sol puede estar muy contenta por (OR durante) una semana en Cabo San Lucas.

9 Direct Object Pronouns

9·1
1. lo
2. la
3. los
4. la
5. la
6. los
7. la
8. los
9. lo
10. lo
11. lo
12. lo
13. los
14. las
15. la

9·2
1. Te amo. OR Te quiero.
2. Lo amo. OR Lo quiero.
3. Él me ama. OR Él me quiere.
4. Te veo.
5. Lo conozco. OR La conozco.
6. Ella lo ve.
7. Lo bebo.
8. La tengo.
9. Lo tienes.
10. Ella los tiene.
11. Me amas. OR Me quieres.
12. Lo odio.
13. Ellos nos aman. OR Ellos nos quieren.
14. Me ves.
15. Me conocéis.
16. La vemos.
17. La comen.
18. Lo quiero.
19. La queremos.
20. Las tenemos.

9·3
1. La compro en… (*Answer will vary.*)
2. Los compro en… (*Answer will vary.*)
3. Lo estudio en… (*Answer will vary.*)
4. Sí, lo conozco.
5. Sí, lo tomo.
6. Sí, la comprendo.
7. Sí, la leo.
8. Sí, lo leo.
9. Sí, la hago.
10. Sí, la conozco.
11. Sí, las veo.
12. Sí, lo como.
13. Sí, las miro.
14. Sí, los leo.

9·4
1. No lo tengo.
2. No la quiero.
3. No lo conozco.
4. No me conoces.
5. Ellos no la compran.
6. Él no lo escribe.
7. Ellos no los leen.
8. Ella no lo gana.
9. No lo llevo.
10. No te vemos.
11. No la tienes.

12. Ellos no lo ven.
13. Él no me conoce.
14. Ellos no nos conocen.
15. No lo usamos.
16. Ella no lo lee.
17. No las cantamos.
18. Ustedes no lo tienen.
19. Nunca (OR Jamás) los llevas.
20. Nunca (OR Jamás) nos ves.

9·5
1. lavarla
2. comerla
3. escribirlo
4. limpiarla
5. tocarlas
6. bailarlo
7. construirlos
8. verlo
9. conocerla
10. oírla
11. verlo
12. prepararlas
13. oírla
14. conocerlos
15. visitarlo

9·6
1. Él me quiere ver.
2. Ella lo quiere besar.
3. Los debes comer.
4. Ellos lo tienen que hacer.
5. Las queremos conocer.
6. Ella tiene que cantarla.
7. Debo leerlo.
8. Quiero verte mañana.
9. Ellos necesitan tenerlo para mañana.
10. Juan puede vernos.

9·7
1. ¿Quieres verla conmigo?
2. ¿Vas a comerlo?
3. ¿Debemos beberla ahora o debemos ponerla en el refrigerador?
4. ¿Podemos comerlo o debemos tirarlo a la basura?
5. No debes ponerlos en la sala.
6. Si no quieres tenerla, debes ponerla en la caja y devolverla.
7. No puedo llevarlos a una fiesta formal.
8. ¿Por qué no puedes verme?
9. No tienes que hacerlo hoy.
10. ¿Quieres abrirlas en la mañana y cerrarlas en la noche?

9·8
1. No los quiero ver esta noche.
2. No la debes devolver.
3. ¿Por qué no lo puedes decir?
4. No la vamos a ver en la biblioteca.
5. No las puede tirar a la basura. Ella las debe reciclar.
6. ¿Cuándo las puedo ver?
7. Si no lo quieres oír, puedes apagar la radio.
8. ¿Dónde los quieres guardar? ¿Los podemos poner aquí?
9. ¿La van a vender (ustedes)?
10. ¡No, no lo puedes golpear!

9·9   Yo sé que Donald tiene mi dinero, mi edificio, y los muebles dentro del edificio. Él piensa (cree) que no sé esto, pero, sí, yo lo sé. Donald piensa (cree) que (él) es más inteligente que todos, pero no es. Primero, el dinero: Yo sé que él lo tiene porque tengo un documento que dice que él me lo debe. Es un contrato y tiene su firma en la parte inferior de la página del contrato. Segundo, el edificio: Es mío. Otra vez, tengo un contrato con su firma en la parte inferior de la página en que él me lo promete. Día tras día, no recibo nada. Él nunca mantiene su palabra. Tercero, los muebles: Una vez más, yo sé que él tiene mis muebles porque hay fotos de su sala en una revista y está llena de (con) mi sofá, mis sillas mis mesas, y más. Yo sé esto porque son de oro. Él cree que todo es suyo, pero no es la verdad. Estas cosas son mías y yo lo sé. Y las quiero ahora.

10   Indirect Object Pronouns

10·1
1. a lie, me
2. nothing, him
3. food, us
4. meal, us
5. us, friends
6. it (*understood*), you
7. ring, you
8. drinks, everyone
9. letter, note, etc. (*understood*), me
10. diamonds, her

10·2
1. me
2. nos
3. le
4. Les
5. le
6. Le
7. Le
8. Le
9. Me
10. nos
11. les
12. Os
13. Les
14. te
15. le

10·3
1. Le digo la verdad.
2. Él no me dice la verdad. Él me dice una mentira.
3. Le damos las flores, y ella nos da el dinero.
4. Les escribo una carta cada semana.
5. Ellos nos escriben cada mes.
6. Ella le canta una canción.
7. John es mi ayudante y le digo todo.
8. Siempre le digo que es bonita.
9. Les envío (OR mando) una tarjeta para su aniversario.
10. ¿Qué te dan para tu cumpleaños cada año?

10·4
1. Él no me dice nada.
2. Yo no le digo nada.
3. Ellos nunca le envían nada porque no saben su dirección.
4. No le doy dinero porque ella nunca me dice "gracias."
5. El mesero (OR El camarero) no te canta "Feliz cumpleaños."
6. ¿Por qué no le dicen la verdad?
7. ¿Por qué no os compran un portatíl nuevo?
8. Les sirvo la cena, pero nunca me dan las gracias. ¡Qué grosero!
9. Si no me hacen preguntas, no les digo mentiras.
10. No les prestamos dinero.

10·5
1. darle
2. decirles
3. prestarme
4. alquilarles
5. decirte
6. enviarle
7. cantaros

8. decirnos
9. mostrarle
10. contarnos
11. diseñarme
12. prepararles
13. decirles
14. venderles
15. servirnos

10·6
1. Le quiero dar un regalo.
2. Él me necesita decir la verdad.
3. Le debemos escribir una carta.
4. Nos debes escribir más a menudo.
5. Les tienen que decir la verdad.
6. Debemos darles aceite de oliva.
7. Él quiere comprarle un diamante.
8. Cuando él viene a nuestra casa, siempre quiere traernos algo.
9. No puedo enviarte (OR mandarte) estos floreros por correo.
10. Necesitáis decirle algo.

10·7
1. ¿Quieres traerme un gatito? ¿Me quieres traer un gatito?
2. No vamos a mostrarles nuestros últimos hallazgos. No les vamos a mostrar nuestros últimos hallazgos.
3. ¿Quieres venderles estas pinturas? ¿Les quieres vender estas pinturas?
4. ¿Quién va a pagarme el dinero? ¿Quién me va a pagar el dinero?
5. ¿Puedes enviarnos los muebles para el martes? ¿Nos puedes enviar los muebles para el martes?
6. El artista no puede pintarle un cuadro para junio. El artista no le puede pintar un cuadro para junio.
7. No voy a lavarte la ropa. No te voy a lavar la ropa.
8. No queremos decirles (OR contarles) las malas noticias. No les queremos decir (OR contar) las malas noticias.
9. ¿Cuándo podéis construirnos el edificio? ¿Cuándo nos podéis construir el edificio?
10. ¿Debes escribirle tal carta? ¿Le debes escribir tal carta?

10·8
1. Le digo a Juan todo.
2. Quiero decirle todo a él. OR Le quiero decir todo a él.
3. Ella le escribe a su tía cada mes.
4. ¿Por qué le traes tanto a Mateo?
5. Ella le da los documentos a su abogado.
6. Ella tiene que darle el dinero a la policía. OR Ella le tiene que dar el dinero a la policía.
7. ¡Margarita nos regala a nosotros un caballo!
8. ¡Oliver quiere regalarme a mí un reloj de Cartier! OR ¡Oliver me quiere regalar a mí un reloj de Cartier!
9. ¿Qué les haces a tus amigos? Les hago una torta.
10. Les traigo a ellos un periódico cada mañana.
11. Usualmente les compro a ellas ropa para Navidad.
12. ¿Qué debemos comprarle a ella? OR ¿Qué le debemos comprar a ella?
13. Romeo le envía (OR manda) rosas a Julieta en el día de San Valentín.
14. ¿Van a enviarles (OR mandarles) algo a ustedes este año? OR ¿Les van a enviar (OR mandar) algo a ustedes este año?
15. George Washington no puede decirle una mentira a nadie. OR George Washington no le puede decir una mentira a nadie.

10·9
1. Sí, me gusta la leche. OR No, no me gusta la leche.
2. Sí, me gustan los dramas de Shakespeare. OR No, no me gustan los dramas de Shakespeare.
3. Sí, me gusta comer en el coche. OR No, no me gusta comer en el coche.
4. Sí, me gusta limpiar la casa. OR No, no me gusta limpiar la casa.
5. Sí, me gustan los platos exóticos. OR No, no me gustan los platos exóticos.
6. Sí, me gustan las películas de horror. OR No, no me gustan las películas de horror.
7. Sí, me gusta correr. OR No, no me gusta correr.
8. Sí, me gusta memorizar los verbos españoles. OR No, no me gusta memorizar los verbos españoles.
9. Sí, me gustan los mosquitos. OR No, no me gustan los mosquitos.
10. Sí, me gusta conducir en la hora punta. OR No, no me gusta conducir en la hora punta.

10·10　1. Me fascina este libro.
　　　2. No quiero nada más. Me basta esta comida. OR No quiero nada más. Esta comida me basta.
　　　3. A ella le encanta todo.
　　　4. Me disgusta esta película. OR Esta película me disgusta.
　　　5. Me duelen los ojos.
　　　6. A él no le importa nada y no le interesa nada. ¡Qué triste! OR A él nada le importa y nada le interesa. ¡Qué triste!
　　　7. Me falta un botón en mi camisa.
　　　8. ¡Nos encanta tu nueva casa!
　　　9. ¿Qué te molesta?
　　　10. Estas revistas me parecen absurdas.
　　　11. Después de los días de fiesta, a ellos no les sobra dinero.
　　　12. A él le disgusta el café, pero a mí me encanta.
　　　13. Me vuelve loco/loca (OR encanta) esta obra de teatro.
　　　14. No me caen bien las galletas con pasas.
　　　15. A ella le encantan los deportes, pero a él le disgustan.

10·11　A Donna le disgustan sus suegros. Le molestan en toda forma posible. Para empezar, son personas aburridas. A ellos no les interesa ni nada ni nadie, y no tienen amigos porque a ellos no les interesan otras personas. Ellos nunca le hacen una pregunta a Donna ni a nadie. A ella le molestan porque son tan egoístas. A su suegra le fascina las zonas comerciales, y le encanta ir de compras. Su suegro está completamente sumido en sí mismo. A él nada más le importa, menos su próxima comida. A Donna, que tiene muchos amigos y varios intereses, sus suegros le parecen personas trágicas.

11　Reflexive Object Pronouns

11·1　1. Me ducho.
　　　2. Me baño.
　　　3. Te duchas cada día.
　　　4. Él se afeita cada mañana.
　　　5. Ella se cepilla los dientes tres veces al día.
　　　6. Nos cepillamos los dientes.
　　　7. Ellos se afeitan dos veces al día.
　　　8. Él se lava el pelo.
　　　9. Me lavo la cara.
　　　10. Te secas el pelo.
　　　11. Usted se seca con una toalla.
　　　12. Me peino (el pelo) a menudo.
　　　13. Ella se peina (el pelo) casi nunca.
　　　14. Me peso en la báscula de baño.
　　　15. Ella se pesa dos veces al día.

11·2　1. Cuando me pruebo ropa nueva, me veo (OR me miro) en el espejo.
　　　2. ¿A qué hora te acuestas y a qué hora te levantas?
　　　3. Normalmente las personas se casan durante los fines de semana.
　　　4. Me enfermo (OR Me pongo enfermo/enferma) cuando como comida que tiene mucha grasa.
　　　5. Me voy al trabajo cada mañana a las ocho.
　　　6. Me ducho, me cepillo los dientes, me seco el pelo, me visto y después me voy al trabajo.
　　　7. Me pongo enfermo/enferma cuando veo un pelo en la comida.
　　　8. Miss America se desmaya cuando se pone la corona.
　　　9. Cada noche me desvisto, me pongo el pijama, me acuesto y me duermo.
　　　10. Cuando Laura se queda en un hotel, se preocupa por recoger chinches.

11·3

1. me
2. se
3. nos
4. me
5. se
6. se
7. se
8. me
9. te
10. os
11. me
12. se, se

11·4

1. Después de vestirme, me miro en el espejo.
2. Antes de irnos, nos ponemos los abrigos, las manoplas y los sombreros.
3. Después de bañarme, me pongo la bata y me relajo.
4. En vez de ducharme, voy a bañarme esta noche.
5. Este jabón es el mejor para lavarse la cara.
6. Uso este champú para lavarme el pelo.
7. Cuando me quedo en un hotel, siempre pido una llamada para despertarme.
8. Él toma una pastilla cada noche para dormirse.
9. Algunas personas meditan para relajarse.
10. Necesitáis una navaja y una hoja para afeitaros.

11·5

1. Para nuestra luna de miel, queremos quedarnos en un hotel elegante.
2. ¿Dónde van a quedarse en París?
3. Tengo mucho calor. Voy a quitarme el suéter.
4. Tengo mucho frío. Tengo que ponerme el abrigo.
5. Nadie quiere enfermarse, pero desgraciadamente esto ocurre.
6. A nuestro perro le gusta bañarse en la piscina de nuestros vecinos. Nuestro vecino se enoja cuando nuestro perro lo hace.
7. Si quieres lavarte el pelo, hay champú en el gabinete.
8. Si quiere afeitarse, el conserje puede darle una navaja y algunas hojas.
9. Si quieren ponerse bien, tienen que tomar este caldo de pollo.
10. Vas a enfermarte si comes esa carne cruda.

11·6

"¡Él ya no se baña nunca! Es absolutamente terrible." Mi vecina me dice todo, y hoy ella se queja de su esposo. Es una mujer fastidiosa y se queja todo el tiempo. Me dice que debo lavarme el pelo más a menudo. Le digo que eso es mi problema y que ella debe callarse. Me dice que no puede callarse cuando nadie en su familia ni se baña ni se ducha. Me dice que después de acostarse, no puede dormirse porque se preocupa por todas estas personas que no se lavan. Yo le digo que (ella) puede comprarse o un bote de Febreze o una manguera.

12 Double-Object Pronoun Order: RID

12·1

1. Él me lo da.
2. Ella te lo dice.
3. Te lo damos.
4. Te la escribo.
5. Él nos los envía.
6. Te la cantamos.
7. ¿Por qué me lo das?
8. ¿Quién te lo tiene?
9. ¿Cuándo me lo haces?
10. ¿Por qué nos lo dices?
11. Me la preparo.
12. Ella se las compra.

12·2
1. Él se la canta.
2. Se lo decimos.
3. Se los compras.
4. Se lo escribo.
5. (Él) Se los envía.
6. Se lo digo.
7. (Él) Se la vende.
8. Se las das.
9. Nadie se lo dice.
10. ¿Por qué se lo dices?
11. Se las traemos.
12. Ella se lo cocina.
13. Se las hago.
14. ¿Se los haces?
15. ¿Quién se lo da?

12·3
1. Ella no me lo dice.
2. No se lo digo.
3. No nos las compramos.
4. Ellos no nos la envían a tiempo.
5. Ella no nos lo hace cada día.
6. No se la doy.
7. Él no me lo paga en efectivo.
8. Él no me lo da a tiempo.
9. ¿Por qué no se la envías mañana?
10. ¿Se las compras cada día?
11. Nunca me las compro.
12. Nunca se los decimos.

12·4
1. Quiero decírtelo. Te lo quiero decir.
2. Quiero comprártela. Te la quiero comprar.
3. Tienes que dármelo. Me lo tienes que dar.
4. Tenemos que vendértelos. Te los tenemos que vender.
5. Tenemos que vendérselo. Se lo tenemos que vender.
6. Ellos deben comprártelas. Ellos te las deben comprar.
7. Ellos deben comprárselo. Ellos se lo deben comprar.
8. Ella necesita enviármela. Ella me la necesita enviar.
9. (Ustedes) Tienen que dárnosla. (Ustedes) Nos la tienen que dar.
10. Debo traérselo. Se lo debo traer.
11. Ellos deben dármelas. Ellos me las deben dar.
12. Ella quiere cantárnosla. Ella nos la quiere cantar.
13. Puedes enviármelo por correo. Me lo puedes enviar por correo.
14. Él puede pagártela en efectivo. Él te la puede pagar en efectivo.
15. Quiero pagároslos con un cheque. Os los quiero pagar con un cheque.

12·5
1. ¿Puedes hacérmelo? ¿Me lo puedes hacer?
2. No, no puedo hacértelo. No, no te lo puedo hacer.
3. ¿Tenemos que decírsela? ¿Se la tenemos que decir?
4. ¿Cuándo quieres dárselas? ¿Cuándo se las quieres dar?
5. No necesitas pagármelo ahora. No me lo necesitas pagar ahora.
6. Ellos no pueden vendértelo en los Estados Unidos. Ellos no te lo pueden vender en los Estados Unidos.
7. No podemos vendérsela a este precio. No se la podemos vender a este precio.
8. ¿Cuándo quieres decírmelo? ¿Cuándo me lo quieres decir?
9. ¿No vas a traérnoslo hoy? ¿No nos lo vas a traer hoy?
10. ¿No pueden enviárnoslas por correo? ¿No nos las pueden enviar por correo?

12·6   Cada año recibo muchos regalos para mi cumpleaños. Tengo muchos amigos que tienen tiendas y (ellos) siempre me regalan (OR dan) lo que venden o lo que hacen. Y para sus cumpleaños yo les doy regalos también. Mi amigo Merlín vende flores, y me las regala (OR da). Manolo vende zapatos y me los regala (OR da). Juan vende café y me lo regala (OR da). Oribe vende champú y me lo regala (OR da). Coco hace perfume y me lo envía (OR manda) porque vive en Francia. Stella hace vestidos y me los envía (OR manda). Harry hace joyas y siempre me hace algo especial para mi cumpleaños. Este año quiero un avión privado. ¿Quién va a regalármelo? (OR ¿Quién me lo va a regalar?)

13   Reciprocal Pronouns

13·1   1. Nos, We know each other (OR one another) very well.
2. se, They love each other (OR one another) a lot.
3. Os, You all see each other (OR one another) through the window.
4. Se, Do you know each other (OR one another)?
5. Se, They (OR You) kiss each other every morning.
6. nos, Every day we tell each other "I love you."
7. se, When they are angry, they don't speak (OR talk) to each other.
8. Os, Do you all visit each other (OR one another) often?
9. se, se, They fight (with each other) a lot, because they hate each other.
10. Nos, We speak (OR talk) to each other on the telephone three times every week.
11. se, They want to know each other (OR one another) better.
12. nos, We can't see each other (OR one another) as often as we want.

13·2   1. Nos escribimos cartas largas cada semana.
2. ¿Cuándo os veis?
3. ¿Por qué se gritan tanto?
4. Los tórtolos se cantan en la copa del árbol.
5. Nos compramos regalos cada diciembre.
6. Los cinco amigos se encuentran en el gimnasio cada viernes por la tarde.
7. No podemos hablarnos porque mi teléfono celular no funciona.
8. No deben decirse todo. Él no puede guardar un secreto.
9. Podéis miraros ahora.
10. Mis vecinos se gritan cada sábado por la noche.

13·3   Voy a la reunión de mi escuela secundaria en dos semanas. Estoy muy ilusionada porque Enrique va a asistir. Yo sé esto porque mi mejor amiga, Laura, es la secretaria de la clase. Ella y yo nos hablamos cada semana y (ella) me dice (OR cuenta) todo. Estas reuniones son delicadas. Queremos vernos, pero al mismo tiempo no queremos vernos. O, tal vez, queremos vernos en el pasado, lo cual ya no existe. Es especialmente difícil para las parejas románticas. Unas parejas previas se ven después de muchos años y es maravilloso. Pero hay otras ex-parejas que se ven y es una experiencia horrible.

14   The Pronoun **Se** and the Passive Voice

14·1   1. vende   6. exportan
2. come   7. baila
3. hacen   8. fabrican
4. bailan   9. liman
5. cultivan   10. fabrica

14·2   *Answers may vary.*
1. Se habla español aquí.
2. Se hablan español y francés aquí.
3. Se venden zapatos allí.
4. No se venden fuegos artificiales y los licores a los adolescentes. OR Los fuegos artificiales y los licores no se venden a los adolescentes.
5. No se permite la entrada antes de las diez. OR La entrada no se permite antes de las diez.
6. No se permiten las cámaras en el teatro. OR Las cámaras no se permiten en el teatro.
7. El oro y las joyas no se consideran buenas inversiones.
8. Los restaurantes y los museos se cierran los lunes.
9. El banco se cierra a las dos y media.
10. Se fabrican piñatas en esta fábrica.

14·3   *Answers may vary.*
1. Se debe pagar los impuestos cada abril.
2. No se puede estar en dos lugares al mismo tiempo.
3. Se necesita cambiar el aceite en el coche cada tres mil millas.
4. No se debe culpar a los otros (OR a los demás) por los resultados de sus acciones.
5. Se debe hacer ejercicio y meditar diariamente.
6. Se debe hacer más claros estos mapas. ¡No se puede leer esto!
7. No se puede extraer la sangre de un nabo.
8. No se puede juzgar un libro por su portada.
9. Se debe cepillar los dientes después de comer y antes de acostarse.
10. Se puede nadar y jugar al tenis en este club.
11. Para bailar La Bamba, se necesita una poca de gracia.
12. Nunca se explicaron los OVNIs.
13. ¿Se puede entrar? ¿A qué hora se abren las puertas?
14. En esta tienda se paga un precio fijo.
15. Se dice que se debe mirar antes de saltar.

14·4
1. El centro comercial se cierra a las nueve y media.
2. Se enoja cuando se paga una fortuna para ver una película y se sienta enfrente de idiotas que hablan sin cesar.
3. Usualmente, las bombillas se queman después de cien horas.
4. Cuando se estropea un coche en la autopista, es un catástrofe para todos.
5. ¿A qué hora se abre ese restaurante?
6. El sol se pone a las ocho y media de la noche en el verano.
7. Con este aparato, las luces se encienden y se apagan automáticamente.
8. Después de los días de fiesta, se rompen millones de juguetes.
9. Cuando ella canta, se quiebran todos los vasos.
10. Los museos se cierran a las seis en punto.

14·5   Quiero ir a Madrid para mis próximas vacaciones. Tengo un folleto conmigo ahora. ¡A ver! ¿Qué se puede hacer en Madrid? Se dice aquí que el Prado es uno de los mejores museos del mundo y que se puede pasar varios días explorando sus tesoros. Se dice que en Madrid el sistema del metro es muy bueno, así que no se necesita alquilar un coche. Se puede tomar el metro a todos los sitios en la ciudad. Si se va a un buen restaurante en Madrid, se puede probar el cochinillo asado. También, El Retiro es un parque precioso y se puede alquilar barquitos para recorrer el estanque. Se puede asistir a las corridas porque España es uno de los pocos países en los que todavía es legal, y se puede bailar hasta las cinco de la mañana. ¡Se puede hacer de todo en esta ciudad maravillosa!

II PREPOSITIONS

15 Prepositions and Prepositional Phrases

15·1
1. Él siempre habla acerca de su novia.
2. Prefiero el café con leche y azúcar.
3. Él prefiere el té sin azúcar.
4. *Don Quijote* es la mejor novela del mundo, según José.
5. Además de flores, su novio le da dulces en cada cita.
6. La espalda del director está contra la pared.
7. Este libro es sobre George Washington.
8. Ellos no escriben mucho acerca de sus problemas.
9. ¿Quieres la pizza con carne o sin carne?
10. Me gusta todo aquí excepto (OR salvo OR menos) los zapatos.
11. Su tesis es sobre el arte de Roma.
12. Según Julia, sus amigos no saben nada acerca de la música clásica.
13. Quiero todo contra la pared, menos (OR salvo OR excepto) el podio.
14. Tienes que servir las bebidas además de la comida.
15. La biblioteca no tiene nada sobre la historia de la pizza.

15·2
1. Hay un libro encima de la mesa.
2. Juan está a la derecha de mí y Felipe está a la izquierda de Elena.
3. ¿Vives al lado de nuestro restaurante?
4. Cada primavera sembramos flores delante de la casa.
5. Necesitamos más iluminación sobre los cuadros.
6. La gente a través del país mira los juegos olímpicos en la televisión.
7. Mi canción favorita es "Cerca de ti."
8. Muchas personas quieren (OR Mucha gente quiere) vivir lejos del aeropuerto.
9. ¿Sabes que hay un tigre debajo de tu cama?
10. ¿Por qué hay tantos perros fuera de tu casa?
11. ¿Quién está en la cocina con Dinah?
12. ¿Qué tienes dentro de la boca?
13. Él trabaja en el banco.
14. Ellos están en el banco.
15. No hay nada en la televisión esta noche.
16. No hay nada entre nosotros.
17. ¿Quién está detrás de ti?
18. Se ven (OR miran) las películas en el cine.

15·3
1. a lo largo de
2. más allá de
3. alrededor de
4. por
5. hacia
6. a lo largo de
7. hacia
8. por
9. más allá de
10. alrededor de

15·4
1. Corro alrededor del lago cada mañana.
2. ¿Caminas (or Andas) a lo largo del bulevar?
3. El detective busca por la casa.
4. Él siempre mira hacia sus metas.
5. Superman puede volar por el aire.
6. Cada noche, caminan (or andan) por el centro comercial.
7. Si miras más allá de ese árbol, puedes ver la montaña rusa.
8. ¿Quieres caminar (or andar) alrededor de la cuadra conmigo?
9. No puedes ir más allá del final de esta cuadra.
10. Podemos conducir hacia el río y después caminar (or andar) a lo largo de la senda.
11. Nathan Chen puede patinar hacia adelante y hacia atrás.
12. Superman puede volar, pero no vuela hacia atrás.

15·5
1. Iowa está al norte de Missouri.
2. Arkansas está al sur de Missouri.
3. Kansas está al oeste de Missouri.
4. Illinois está al este de Missouri.
5. Michigan está al nordeste (or noreste) de Missouri.
6. Nebraska está al noroeste de Missouri.
7. Oklahoma está al suroeste (or sudoeste) de Missouri.
8. Tennessee está al sureste (or sudeste) de Missouri.
9. Louisiana está al sur de Missouri.
10. Minnesota está al norte de Missouri.

15·6
1. A causa de (or Por) la pandemia del COVID-19, no puedo ir al cine con mis amigos.
2. Leo (or Estoy leyendo) un libro de (or por) John Steinbeck.
3. Este libro es para ustedes.
4. ¡Saludos desde Cancún!
5. Vamos al centro comercial. ¿Quieres ir con nosotros?
6. Estas perlas son de Japón.
7. Todos mis amigos de la universidad están aquí.
8. ¿Qué quieren de mí?
9. No tengo nada para ti.
10. Él me llama desde Alemania cada semana.
11. Por (or A causa de) su actitud y amargura, él no tiene amigos.
12. La novela *Les Miserables* es por (or de) Victor Hugo.
13. Marchamos (or Estamos marchando) a Pretoria.
14. ¡Uno de ellos va a ganar el premio gordo!
15. Estoy cansado/cansada, y por esta razón voy a dormir una siesta.

15·7
1. después de
2. durante
3. hasta
4. Antes de
5. desde
6. a
7. después de
8. durante
9. antes de
10. durante
11. después de
12. por

15·8
1. No tienes que estar aquí hasta mañana.
2. Necesito limpiar el garaje antes del invierno.
3. Hace frío, ¿no? Sí. Desde el martes.
4. Algunas personas creen que los fantasmas viven después de la muerte.

5. Después de la cena, siempre lavamos los platos.
6. ¿Qué quieres hacer durante nuestro descanso?
7. Usualmente, ¿qué haces por la tarde?
8. ¿Qué quieres hacer antes del baile?
9. Usualmente hablamos durante los anuncios.
10. Él va a trabajar aquí hasta marzo.
11. ¿No tienes leche? No. No desde el sábado.
12. Ellos trabajan de lunes a viernes.
13. Podemos mirar la película e ir al restaurante después.
14. Siempre pico las cebollas antes de cocinarlas.

16   Para and Por

16·1
1. g
2. b
3. f
4. c
5. j
6. f
7. d
8. a
9. i
10. e
11. j
12. d
13. i
14. j
15. b
16. e
17. h
18. c
19. a
20. i

16·2
1. Esta casa es perfecta para nosotros.
2. Necesitamos una mesa nueva para el comedor.
3. Para algunas personas, no es importante tener un coche.
4. Estos zapatos son para bailar el tango.
5. Tienes que leer este libro para el jueves.
6. Él mira la televisión para evitar sus problemas.
7. Salgo para África mañana.
8. Estudio para mago.
9. Él es muy cortés para un adolescente.
10. ¿Puedes escribir la carta para el martes?
11. Esta comida es para el gato.
12. Para él, el invierno es maravilloso, pero para mí, el verano es la mejor estación.
13. Ella trabaja mucho para sacar buenas notas.
14. ¿A qué hora sales para el trabajo?
15. Estas manzanas no son para comer.

16·3
1. a
2. j
3. m
4. d
5. c
6. o
7. n
8. b
9. f
10. g
11. e
12. l
13. i
14. h
15. b
16. d
17. o
18. m
19. k
20. e
21. h
22. j
23. i
24. f
25. g

16·4 1. Vamos a la escuela (OR al colegio) por autobús.
2. Puedes tener esos zapatos por diez dólares.
3. Él tiene por lo menos veinte gatos.
4. Cuando viajo, siempre camino por la ciudad e investigo todo.
5. Leemos el periódico por treinta minutos cada mañana.
6. Juanita está enferma hoy. ¿Puedes trabajar por ella?
7. Voy al supermercado por leche, mantequilla y huevos.
8. Cada lunes por la noche él mira (el) fútbol americano en la televisión.
9. Por sus alergias, no puede tocar el gato.
10. Gracias por nada.
11. Por dar tanto a los otros (OR a los demás), ella merece una medalla.
12. El noventa por ciento de todos los dentistas dicen que esta pasta de dientes es horrible.
13. Él viene por mi casa de vez en cuando.
14. Sólo tengo estimación por ti.
15. Ahora entiendo las diferencias entre *por* y *para* por primera vez.
16. Puedes enviarme los contratos por fax.

16·5 1. para, recipient of an item or action
2. para, comparison to a certain standard
3. por, expresses thanks
4. por, duration of time
5. por, indicates motion, through, around
6. para, time limit of an action
7. para, recipient of an item or action
8. por, por, por, used before periods of the 24-hour day
9. para, destination
10. por, por, means of transportation
11. por, expresses exchange, price
12. para, expresses final destination
13. por, idiomatic expression
14. por, tells why something is a certain way
15. para, in order to do something
16. por, on behalf of
17. por, expresses *per*
18. por, idiomatic expression
19. para, expresses an opinion
20. por, shows point of temporary stop
21. por, shows emotion
22. para, in order to do something, for the purpose of
23. por, expresses "because of"
24. por, tells why something is a certain way
25. por, expresses means of information
26. por, idiomatic expression
27. para, in order to
28. por, used before periods in the 24-hour day
29. por, expresses *per*
30. para, time limit of an action

16·6 *Answers will vary.*
1. a. You can have my shirt for your skirt.
     Destination: Figuratively, "to go with"
   b. You can have my shirt for your skirt.
     Substitution: An equal exchange
2. a. We're going to their house tonight.
     Destination: The implication is that we will stay for a while.
   b. We're going by their house tonight.
     Movement: The implication is that their house is a temporary stop.

3. a. I have lots of shampoo and soap samples for the trip.
        Deadline: The trip is in the future.
    b. I have lots of shampoo and soap samples because of the trip.
        Motivation: "Because of"
4. a. I have many gifts for Daisy and for Lily.
        Destination: Recipient of an action—The gifts are *for* them.
    b. I have a lot of love for Daisy and for Lily.
        Emotions: Tells of one's feelings
5. a. Maksim dances for Derek.
        Destination: Recipient of an action—Maksim's dancing is for Derek, who is watching, being entertained.
    b. Maksim dances for Derek.
        Substitution: Maksim is dancing on behalf of Derek, who can't dance for some reason.
6. a. We're driving to the park.
        Destination: The park is our final destination.
    b. We're driving through (OR throughout) the park.
        Movement: We're moving in (OR within) an area.
7. a. These creams are for allergies.
        Destination: Allergies are an imagined destination.
    b. These allergies are because of the creams.
        Motivation: Tells why the allergies exist
8. a. In my opinion, this soup is spoiled (OR bad).
        Standard: Personal opinion
    b. Because of me this soup is spoiled (OR bad).
        Motivation: Tells why the soup has gone bad

16·7 Ésta es una situación que afecta a todos: La pandemia del nuevo coronavirus, o COVID-19, el acrónimo del coronavirus-19. Produce síntomas similares a los del gripe o la influenza, e incluye fiebre, tos, mialgia, y fatiga. En los casos graves se caracteriza por la neumonía, dificultad de respirar, sepsis o shock séptico. Más de dos millones de personas han muerto en todo el mundo, y continúa propagándose. El país con el peor récord de manejo de la pandemia es los Estados Unidos donde más de medio millón de personas han muerto, sin un final a la vista. Los países con las mejores respuestas a la pandemia, y por eso, las tasas de mortalidad más bajas, incluyen Taiwán, Singapur, y Neo Zelandia. En cada uno de estos países, los lideres la han tomado la pandemia en serio y han ordenado precauciones que incluyen usar máscaras en público, evitar las multitudes, mantener la distancia social, y lavarse las manos. Mientras que éstas son cosas simples, unas personas creen que son difíciles e innecesarias. Pero nada es más difícil que la muerte. La buena noticia es que ahora hay vacunas que protegen a la población, y que el nuevo Presidente, Joe Biden, considera la erradicación de COVID-19 su prioridad número uno.

17 Prepositions and Verbs

17·1
1. Agradezco todo.
2. ¿Qué buscas? Busco mis anteojos.
3. ¿Dónde debemos colgar nuestros abrigos?
4. Me gusta escuchar la música clásica.
5. Puedes apagar las luces porque nos acostamos (OR vamos a acostarnos) ahora.
6. La niñera recoge los juguetes.
7. Él borra todos sus errores.
8. Esta noche Carlota va a salir con Guillermo. Está muy ilusionada.
9. Yo siempre saco la basura. Tú debes sacar la basura de vez en cuando.
10. El abogado entrega la evidencia al juez.
11. Los trapos empapan el aceite.
12. El conductor pisa el freno.
13. Necesito más dinero. Voy a pedir un aumento mañana.
14. ¿Por cuánto tiempo tenemos que esperar el autobús?
15. Puedes encender las luces aquí y apagar las luces allá.

17·2
1. Vamos a conducir (OR manejar) a Vermont en vez de (OR en lugar de) volar.
2. Antes de comprar los huevos, debes mirar dentro del cartón.
3. Siempre me siento mejor después de hacer ejercicio.
4. Además de poder volar, Superman puede ver a través de las paredes.
5. Pienso en escribir una novela.
6. Para llegar al banco, debes doblar a la derecha en la avenida Park.
7. ¿Quieres nadar en vez de (OR en lugar de) jugar al golf?
8. Ella siempre come una barra de proteína después de nadar.
9. ¿Qué tienes que hacer antes de salir?
10. Voy a una conferencia sobre usar computadoras.
11. ¡Además de hervir el agua, esta estufa puede hervir la leche!
12. John tiene que tomar otras tres clases para graduarse.

17·3
1. Esto me suena a mentira.
2. Ella rompe a llorar cada vez que recuerda el dolor de su niñez.
3. Él va a renunciar a su trabajo porque su compañía va a empezar a recortar el personal.
4. Tarde o temprano, tienes que resignarte al hecho de que algunas personas no son honradas.
5. No puedes obligarnos a hacer nada que no queremos hacer.
6. Benjamín da cuerda a su reloj cada día a las nueve de la mañana.
7. La Sra. Dalí anima a sus hijos a estudiar las bellas artes.
8. En esta casa nos sentamos a cenar a las siete en punto.
9. ¿A qué hora subimos al tren?
10. Esta rana sabe a un sapo.
11. Mateo dice que la carne de culebra sabe a pollo.
12. Oscar Wilde dice que puede resistirse a todo salvo a la tentación.
13. En esta sección del libro, aprendemos a usar los verbos que toman la preposición *a*.
14. Algunos atletas se acostumbran a recibir y a gastar mucho dinero.
15. Ricardo no se dispone a darnos nada hoy. No está de humor.

17·4
1. Puedes contar conmigo, pero, ¿puedo contar contigo?
2. Cada miércoles, me encuentro con Kay para cenar y (para) conversar.
3. En la película *Spiderman*, Peter Parker (Spiderman) sale con Mary Jane Watson.
4. Me asusto con la oscuridad durante una tormenta.
5. Es trágico, pero a veces una persona necesita romper con su familia.
6. El egoísta sueña con ser famoso, popular, rico y poderoso.
7. No me asocio con compañías que venden tabaco.
8. De vez en cuando me equivoco con las personas.
9. Siempre nos divertimos con nuestros vecinos.
10. Ella se enfada (OR se enoja) conmigo cuando llego tarde.
11. Donna no se trata con la familia de su esposo porque ellos son personas horribles.
12. Si limpias la bañera con el ácido, vas a dañarla.
13. De vez en cuando me doy con alguien que verdaderamente me inspira.
14. Si Juan no tiene cuidado, va a tropezarse con la pared.
15. Los domingos por la mañana, me contento a menudo con zumo (OR jugo) de naranja y el periódico.

17·5
1. Él siempre se olvida de tomar su medicina.
2. Este sofá sirve de una cama cómoda.
3. Tenemos que terminar de limpiar la casa para las cuatro y media.
4. Cada día me libro de cinco cosas por lo menos porque no me gusta el desorden.
5. Ella siempre se queja de trabajar tanto.
6. Me maravillo de las personas que pueden bailar bien.
7. Estoy encargado/encargada de cocinar y (tú) estás encargado/encargada de servir las comidas.
8. Con frecuencia me olvido del nombre de una persona, pero nunca me olvido de la cara.
9. Debes alejarte de personas peligrosas.
10. Acabo de leer un artículo maravilloso en el periódico.
11. ¿No tenemos jugo de naranja? Me muero de sed.
12. ¿Quién va a cuidar de tu casa la semana que viene?

13. Ellos hablan de mudarse a Troy, New York, el año que viene.
14. No me gusta estar con él porque siempre habla mal de otras personas.
15. Hay personas que abusan de otros (or de los demás) sin remordimiento. Se llaman depredadores sociales.

17·6
1. Algunas personas persisten en hacer ejercicio aun cuando están enfermas y no deben hacerlo.
2. María se complace en tocar la guitarra en las fiestas.
3. Primero pienso en la comida y después pienso en comer algo en particular.
4. Cada día debemos reflexionar en algo bueno de este mundo.
5. A finales del mes, Marcos siempre se ve en un apuro.
6. Cuando llega la policía, el ladrón consiente en ir con ellos pacíficamente.
7. Las personas que chismean se meten en la vida de otras personas.
8. Juan y María quedan (OR convienen) en consultar a un psiquiatra.
9. Cada año quedo en donar dinero a la Sociedad de Cáncer.
10. No debes meterte en sus problemas.
11. No estoy pensando (OR pienso) en nada ahora.
12. Mi hermana nunca se molesta en llamar(me) por teléfono.
13. Me intereso mucho en la política internacional.
14. Tardo una hora en conducir (OR manejar) al estadio de aquí.
15. Para hacer ejercicio, los niños montan en bicicleta.

17·7
1. Usualmente es muy tarde cuando me siento para estudiar.
2. Martha Stewart dice que muchas cosas en la basura sirven para decoraciones en la casa.
3. ¿Están listos/listas para salir (OR irse)? Sí, estamos listos/listas para salir (OR irnos).
4. Estamos para almorzar.
5. Quiero trabajar para otra compañía.
6. ¿Quieres quedarte para mirar las noticias conmigo?
7. Esta película no sirve para nada.
8. Cada enero muchas personas trabajan para perder peso.
9. Kate necesita por lo menos dos horas para prepararse para cada aparición pública.
10. Mike se prepara para encontrar un nuevo trabajo porque trabaja para un verdadero bruto.

17·8
1. Harold se preocupa por perder los dientes y el pelo.
2. En *Anna Karenina,* Levin lucha siempre por hacer lo correcto.
3. El pueblo de Argentina no debe llorar por Evita.
4. Yo miro (OR me preocupo) mucho por el calentamiento global.
5. Muchas personas se ofenden por el desperdicio de comida en los restaurantes.
6. Me muero por ver tu nuevo peinado.
7. En esta oficina, clasificamos todo por tamaño.
8. Usualmente un/una gimnasta termina por hacer algo espectacular.
9. Ellos siempre optan por nadar en el río.
10. Cuando tengo una elección entre dos películas, usualmente opto por la que tiene las mejores reseñas.
11. Laura se impacienta por mudarse a otra parte del país.
12. Muchos abogados defensores abogan por una persona culpable.
13. Te damos (las) gracias por decirnos la verdad.
14. Yo siempre clasifico mis libros por orden alfabético.
15. Ella siempre vota por el candidato menos atractivo.

ABOUT THE AUTHOR

Dorothy Richmond is a Spanish instructor and the author of several Spanish texts and reference works. Titles with McGraw-Hill include *Guide to Spanish Suffixes, The Big Red Book of Spanish Vocabulary* (coauthor), and the following titles in the "Practice Makes Perfect" series: *Spanish Verb Tenses* (first through fourth editions), *Spanish Pronouns and Prepositions* (first through fourth editions), *Spanish Vocabulary* (first through third editions), *Basic Spanish* (first through third editions), and *Spanish Vocabulary Building with Suffixes*. Dorothy Richmond holds degrees in Linguistics, Philosophy, and Educational Administration. She lives in Minneapolis, Minnesota.